AF615103

Air

Once in the air, the YF-22A displays its similarity in configuration to the F-15 Eagle, the main type it will replace in USAF service. Note the cut-back rear fuselage between the fins for the engine exhausts. (Lockheed)

Power 2000

Michael J. Gething

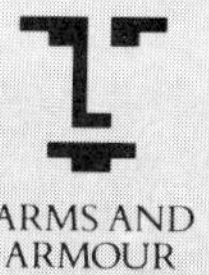

ARMS AND ARMOUR

First published in Great Britain in 1992 by Arms and Armour Press, Villiers House, 41–47 Strand, London WC2N 5JE.

Distributed in the USA by Sterling Publishing Co. Inc., 387 Park Avenue South, New York, NY 10016-8810.

Distributed in Australia by Capricorn Link (Australia) Pty. Ltd., P.O. Box 665, Lane Cove, New South Wales 2066

British Library Cataloguing in Publication Data:
Gething, Michael J.
Air Power 2000
I. Title
623.746
ISBN 185409047X

Designed and edited by DAG Publications Ltd. Designed by David Gibbons; edited by Roger Chesneau; typeset by Wyvern Typesetting Ltd., Bristol; camerawork by M&E Reproductions, North Fambridge, Essex; printed and bound in Great Britain

►
The latest version of the McDonnell Douglas Helicopter Company's AH-64 Apache is the Longbow Apache, which features a millimetre-wave fire control radar mounted above the main rotor spindle and a new variant of the Rockwell AGM-114 Hellfire anti-tank missile. Further improvements are on the horizon. (MDHC)

CONTENTS

In his opening address to a conference on the theme 'Air Power in the Next Generation' held at the University of Southampton in April 1977, the then Chief of the Defence Staff, Marshal of the Royal Air Force Sir Neil Cameron, noted that 'as far as air power is concerned, we must not measure its future against an apparently stable scenario: that might just melt away as we watch it'.

This book was begun in 1990 and completed in July 1991. Since mid-1989 the world had seen such 'an apparently stable scenario ... just melt away'. And we *all* watched it! On our television screens, we nightly witnessed the rise of 'people power' in hard-line Eastern Bloc countries and the sweeping away of the former loyalties to the USSR. Perhaps the most emotive scenes to be seen – which brought the message of change to the man in the street – were those involving the breaching of the Berlin Wall and its subsequent dismantling. The violent overthrow and swift execution of President Nicolae Ceausescu of Romania, and his wife Elena, in Bucharest on Christmas Day 1989, were emotive in themselves, but their implications did not register with the majority of the British public.

The political leaders of the world's two major alliances – NATO and the former Warsaw Pact – are still grappling with the aftermath of these events. Peace is breaking out in Central Europe, and the fallout from this momentous event will be affecting military power on land, by sea and in the air for some time to come.

However, if the 'Cold War' has now become the 'Warm Peace', we must not become complacent. Great Britain did become so once before and almost paid the price. These words are being written just over 50 years after the Battle of Britain, at a time when the memories of those days are refreshed in the minds of those who remember and recounted to those of us (myself included) who came after the dark days of the Second World War. Whatever may come of the thaw in East–West relationships in the ensuing years, it is a sad truth that mankind will, eventually, resort to resolving disputes by means of violence. The civil war in Yugoslavia is indicative of this basic truth. The need for armed forces of one sort or another will not totally recede in the lifetime of this author.

So, just as we were beginning the adjustment to a new era, events in the Middle East caused the biggest build-up of military forces in another country since the Vietnam War and the biggest air movement of men and matériel since the Berlin Airlift of 1948–49. Hostilities between Iraq and the 'rest of the world' finally broke out on the night of 16 January 1991. In an air campaign of an intensity the world has never known, the devastating effect of modern air power was demonstrated, hour-by-hour, on the television screens of the world. Although air power, in total isolation, can never win a war outright, the Gulf War of 1991 almost managed to achieve that objective. At the very least, it allowed the ground forces to achieve their objectives – the liberation of Kuwait and the removal of an immediate Iraqi threat – in short order. President Bush coined the phrase 'The Hundred-Hour War'. Air power was responsible for the swiftness of the ground war.

To return to Sir Neil Cameron's opening address to that conference, he notes that if we wish to look at the future, we can learn much from the past. He sagely observes that '... in the history of air power, the constant has been – paradoxically – that of change'. Flexibility is a marvellous attribute and, thus, I trust that I am flexible enough to look to the future of air power in the light of the changes in world circumstances and the shift in relationships. When this book (and its companion titles in the series) were planned, the odds against seeing the Berlin Wall dismantled in 1990 must have been very long. This volume was planned, and indeed in part written, in what we now see as the closing months of the 'Cold War'. The hard technical facts which will shape the future of air power into the next century cannot change. How the scenario affects the application of the technology is a different matter. Explaining how air power can change is relatively simple: quantifying the degree to which it will change is fraught with difficulties.

As the commonly quoted cliché runs, 'the impossible we do every day; miracles take a little longer'. I trust that this book will go some way to explaining the 'impossible' to the informed layman. As for the 'miracle' of prediction, I can but use my accumulated experience of nineteen years as an aviation and defence journalist to identify possible trends and solutions. Thus I end my Preface with an author's obligatory caveat. I have sought advice, listened to opinions from

▶
Panavia's Tornado Interdictor Strike (IDS) version, known by the RAF as the GR.1 and seen here in Saudi Arabian markings, has already begun an improvement programme. Germany has developed the Electronic Combat and Reconnaissance (ECR) version, while the RAF is to upgrade its GR.1s to GR.4 configuration. (BAe)

AUTHOR'S PREFACE

sources whose expertise is far in excess of my own, sipped more than one bottle of medicinal elderberry wine and pondered over many pipefuls of tobacco as I have drawn my conclusions. These remain my own and, perhaps, posterity may see them vindicated ... or not, as the case may prove.

The compilation of this book has been immensely interesting, drawing as it does on many diverse areas and disciplines. Some of the chapters began life as features for *Defence* magazine and I acknowledge the Editor's permission to use them as a starting point for this book. However, free from the restrictions of space and short deadlines, I have been able to expand areas with either new or more information.

If I were to summarize the future of air power now, it would be to say that it is going to change in the balance of forces but it will not, in the foreseeable future, be declared redundant. Operation 'Desert Storm' proved the need for air power. That said, turn the pages and enjoy them. Science Fiction is fast becoming science fact.

Acknowledgements

To the many experts and engineers of the world's aerospace and defence industries and the serving officers of many armed forces I have spoken with over many years, I would like to express my thanks. I have listened to what you have told me and, I hope, drawn the right conclusions. I also thank my colleagues, past and present, on *Defence* magazine and other members of the world's most exclusive club, 'The Defence Media'. I have lost count of the number of bars in which we have 'chewed the fat' over issues of the time. Specifically, I am grateful to Don Parry, Antony Preston, Martin Streetly and Mike Witt for clarifying many complex issues at one time or another. Finally, acknowledgement is due to my long-suffering wife, Carol, and my children, David and Charlotte. Their forebearance, sometimes under pressure, in allowing me to complete this book is greatly appreciated. Thank you.

Michael J. Gething

INTRODUCTION

The first military application of air craft occurred on 10 April 1794, when Captain Jean-Marie-Joseph Coutelle of the French Republican Army used a captive balloon at Mauberge to overlook Austrian positions, professionally relaying valuable information concerning enemy artillery and working parties. It was used once more during the Battle of Fleurus on 25–26 June and, indeed, many sources declare this the first military use of the balloon. Military aviation had begun.

The use of heavier-than-air craft for military purposes began in 1911, when the Italians used nine aeroplanes for bombing and reconnaissance against the Turks in Libya. By 1918, the First World War had brought air power to a major pinnacle of achievement, with the use of military aircraft in most of the major combat roles we know today – air defence, ground attack, air interdiction, maritime strike, anti-submarine warfare and reconnaissance. The period between the two world wars brought military air transport into the arena and the period after the Second World War saw the introduction of the helicopter, with its own specialized roles running parallel with the tasks already outlined and its establishment in large-scale military use during the Vietnam War.

The reality of modern air warfare was made obvious to the world with the Arab–Israeli 'Six-Day War' of 1967, when it became apparent that wars were fought and won (or lost) with the equipment in service at the outbreak of hostilities. The Falklands campaign of 1982 emphasized the point. The way in which forces were deployed to the Arabian Peninsula immediately following the invasion of Kuwait in August 1990 and the subsequent, successful prosecution of Operation 'Desert Storm' proved it.

However effective the aircraft (or tank or warship) due to enter service next year is claimed to be, it can never be in service in time to affect the outcome of the war being fought today. So, to look at air power in the year 2000, one must begin by looking at where air power is today. The building blocks are already in place and will change little. It is now down to the scenario to shape the future.

Although it may have come to the end of its production run, the Grumman F-14 Tomcat could become a US Navy near-term replacement for the A-12 attack aircraft. An F-14A of VF-102 is illustrated. (CWO2 Joe Leo/USN) ▼

FIXED-WING AIRCRAFT WITH POTENTIAL

Until early in 1990, the scenario against which combat aircraft were designed was one involving a Warsaw Pact move against NATO, and requirements were centred on a European war of high intensity. The events of August 1990 concentrated the mind and the United States, swiftly followed by many other nations, deployed its available forces to meet a new threat in the Arabian Peninsula. Despite the change of threat and modified scenario, the application of air power to deter and then counter the threat was almost 'text-book' in its use. With the advent of the third dimension into the ancient craft of warfare, command of the air has assumed a vitally important position in a country's defence posture. It enables the home base to be secured, from which the armed forces on land, by sea and in the air can move forward to defeat the enemy.

In the maturing years of air warfare, aspects of air power have tended to be exaggerated. Time has proved that, while air power can win battles, it cannot – on its own – win wars. To hold ground means but one thing – soldiers being there, occupying territory. However, in the final decade of the twentieth century, air power has become of equal import as land warfare and sea power: each has its part to to play but, without the other two elements, it can falter.

However, before launching into a look at the aircraft of today, those that will be with us, still, beyond the turn of the century and those that are to come, it is worth considering the roles which fixed-wing air power is called upon to fulfil. A similar look at rotary-wing roles and potential follows in the next chapter.

Roles

Air Defence/Interception In the 1990s, and beyond, air defence has become a highly complex amalgam of elements which range from the operational commander in his bunker out to the fighter pilot in his cockpit, facing the incoming threat. The main components of an air defence system are:

1. A Control and Reporting System, which must provide early warning of the approach of aircraft and also provide the means to direct the defence.
2. Fighter aircraft tasked with the interception and destruction of attacking hostile aircraft before they reach the point of weapons release, preferably as far away from the area being defended as possible.
3. Surface-to-air missiles (SAMs) and anti-aircraft artillery (AAA), integrated with the fighters, with a similar task but at medium and short range, respectively, from the defended area.
4. A communication system between all the components of the air defence system, providing the means to alert, command and control the integrated system.
5. Any complementary operations, such as counter-air strikes, designed to neutralize the enemy's ability to press his attack.

For our purposes, it is the interceptor fighter which concerns us here. Assuming that the earliest possible warning is received (including that provided by airborne early warning, discussed separately below), interceptors must be able to react in time to neutralize the emerging threat. In today's scenario of forward defence, this usually means a mix of aircraft deployed forward to meet the threat, either at forward operating locations (FOLs), where aircraft are held on the ground on quick-reaction alert (QRA), or on combat air patrol (CAP), where a formation (usually a pair) of interceptors flies a 'racetrack' pattern at a point some way towards the area of the expected threat.

Thus interceptor fighters must have 'long legs', including the capability to be refuelled in the air. They must have appropriate sensors to detect the enemy and the equipment to counter any of his electronic emissions. (Indeed, electronic warfare is now indivisible from air warfare, so much so that a separate element has been allocated to the subject.) They must have appropriate weapons, principally air-to-air missiles (AAMs) with 'beyond visual range' (BVR) capability to further the destruction distance but also shorter-range 'dogfight' missiles and guns for close-in combat should this occur. They need the ability to communicate with ground control, with other elements in the air defence network and with themselves, all in a secure way in order to avoid electronic eavesdropping which might give away their plans to the enemy.

At the same time, these interceptors should be capable of high speed while being economical of fuel. More and more they are required to possess 'low observability' or 'stealth' features (again, considered in a separate chapter), to reduce their own probability of detection. They should be reliable and easily maintained, both on the ground and in the air. Finally, wherever possible, it is desirable that the same basic

airframe possess a multi-role capability, in order that production runs can be longer (hence reducing capital expenditure) and spares holdings and support organizations more cost-effective.

That these many conflicting requirements result in aircraft which can do the job continues to amaze me. The solutions will differ from one design team to another, as trade-offs between the varying requirements are made. Apart from technical solutions, economic and political factors can affect the final choice of aircraft. The United States recently chose its new Advanced Tactical Fighter (ATF), the F-22, after evaluating two contenders, the YF-22A, from a team led by Lockheed with input from Boeing and General Dynamics, and the YF-23A, from Northrop teamed with McDonnell Douglas. As requirements get more complex, costs rise and the number of aircraft bought shrink, the major airframe manufacturers have no option but to combine their resources. The ATF competition was a 'winner takes all' affair, of which the contenders are only too painfully aware. The resulting ATF will not be put into production until the middle of the 1990s and will, undoubtedly, be in front-line service for 25 years. If one considers that the current generation of USAF interceptors, the F-15 and F-16, made their maiden flights in 1972 and 1974 respectively, and notes that they will still be with us at the turn of the century, then the indications are that the instruments of air power in the first decade of the twenty-first century will not be much different from what they are today.

Air Superiority This role may be placed on a virtually even footing with that of air defence/interception. Indeed, it is truly 'tactical' and, as such, is the principal driver behind the USAF's ATF programme. Air superiority involves the contest with similar enemy aircraft for command of the sky over any action taking place below, be it on land or by sea. It also involves the destruction of enemy attack, strike or bomber aircraft attempting to influence the battle below. With a secondary air-to-ground capability, the air superiority fighter can also be called upon to contribute to the outcome of the land battle.

Where the demands of air-to-air and air-to-ground are more equally balanced, the term 'air combat fighter' has evolved. Indeed, one can find the roles of air superiority and air defence, together with the more general aspects of battlefield air interdiction, fulfilled by the same basic type in some air forces. Flexibility in application is most important. The F-16 is a typical example. It was developed in the early 1970s as a lightweight fighter technology demonstrator to show exactly what could be achieved at the time. As the demonstration progressed, the USAF discovered that it was unable to afford as many F-15s as it would have liked. The demonstration programme involving the YF-16 was then turned into a contest with its parallel rival, the YF-17, for a lightweight fighter which could be procured at a greatly reduced cost. The plan was for a 'high–low' mix of the two types – fewer of the more sophisticated F-15, more of the lightweight fighter. The F-16 won and was put into production, and, since 1974, it has been progressively developed into an all-weather, day/night fighter/attack aircraft, over 4,500 being ordered for home and export use.

Counter-Air As remarked earlier, counter-air operations may be used as an adjunct to air defence operations. The essence of counter-air is to gain and

◀ The latest version of the McDonnell Douglas F-15 Eagle series is the two-seat F-15E interdictor, which gave an excellent account of itself during the Gulf War. (Texas Instruments)

▶ Equivalent to the F-15 is the Soviet Union's Sukhoi Su-27 'Flanker', seen here during the Farnborough Air Show in 1990. (Author)

maintain a favourable air situation so that hostile air forces are prevented from operating against friendly land, sea and air forces. As such, the counter-air can be fought either offensively or defensively. Offensive operations involve attacks on enemy airfields, missile sites, radar and support installations, or, using fighters, seeking out and attacking hostile aircraft in the air. Defensive counter-air includes all aspects of air defence, and while it does not in itself provide a favourable air situation, it is complementary to offensive counter-air, being designed to destroy hostile aircraft.

Counter-air operations would be used in the opening stages of a conflict against a foe with an effective air force, in order to reduce his capacity for combat and thus induce a favourable air situation. In order to maintain the advantage, counter-air operations may need to be carried out at later stages in the conflict.

Interdiction On the basis that it is more effective to destroy enemy ground forces and supporting matériel (ammunition, fuel and other supplies) before they reach the front line, planned strike/attack bombing operations are used against such rear echelon targets. This is interdiction, which, in its broadest definition, means pre-planned operations against enemy lines of communication on land, sea or air, in order to prevent or severely restrict his movement into, or out of, operational or battle areas. Targets for interdiction would include road and rail bridges, marshalling yards or

◀ Perhaps the most flexible multi-role fighter of the late 1970s and 1980s, with much life remaining, is the General Dynamics F-16 Fighting Falcon. Ordered by nineteen countries (at the time of writing), it is seen here in F-16C form, loaded with Rockeye cluster bombs. (GD, Fort Worth)

◀ The Brazilian/Italian collaboration deal between Alenia, Aermacchi and Embraer has resulted in the compact AMX strike fighter. Several specialized versions are proposed, including a two-seat anti-shipping strike aircraft. (Alenia)

▶ Despite its developmental problems, Rockwell's B-1B Lancer is set to enjoy a longevity comparable to that of its predecessor, the B-52 Stratofortress. (USAF)

vehicle parks, and communications centres. Such operations require careful planning and sustained effort, 24 hours a day, in all weathers. Traditionally, movement down lines of communication has been at night, so such operations would be tasked to hit such targets during the hours of darkness.

Assuming that air superiority has been achieved, then interdiction is a comparatively straightforward operation. However, history has shown us that whatever interdiction efforts are mounted, some supplies will succeed in getting through. Thus continuous pressure should be maintained in these operations and the transfer of interdiction assets to other duties should not be undertaken lightly.

Close Air Support Air attack against targets in close proximity to friendly ground forces constitutes the principal element of close air support (CAS), otherwise known as ground attack operations up to the end of the 1960s. Such operations require detailed integration with the ground forces (knowing their fire and movement plans) in order for CAS to succeed. Another mission is also sometimes associated with CAS – that of Battlefield Air Interdiction (BAI), which is an interdiction-type mission performed very close to the battle area and aimed at the enemy's second echelon forces. Where CAS is flown in support of recently landed forces (by sea and air) and the latter have little by way of artillery, then the CAS aircraft becomes the land

◀ In a joint Anglo-US development, led by McDonnell Douglas, the Harrier was further developed into the AV-8B Harrier II (illustrated). A radar-equipped version, the Harrier II Plus, is now being pursued for the US Marine Corps, Italy and Spain. (MACAIR)

forces' artillery, usually against threat armour. To fly a CAS/BAI mission (sometimes referred to as 'mud-moving') is to fly in the face of hostile ground-to-air defences – missiles and guns of all calibres – and so, unless the need is pressing, such missions will carefully take into account the balance of the enemy's anti-air assets.

The typical example of CAS was the use of RAF rocket-firing Typhoons and Tempests in a 'cab rank' patrol over the advancing Allied forces in 1944–45. Today, the successor to these aircraft comes from the same stable (the Hawker element of British Aerospace) in the form of the Harrier and its Anglo-American development, the Harrier GR.5/7 (or AV-8B).

Strategic Bombing In terms of its importance, this role – the once all-embracing role of air power – has dropped somewhat in the ratings. The reason for this is simple. The cost of developing and maintaining a traditional long-range, heavy bomber force has risen astronomically, so that few nations can afford to retain this luxury. Added to this, the reduction in East–West tension over recent months has negated much of the post-war requirement for such forces. That said, the capability to strike over long (intercontinental) ranges is one worth retaining for as long as possible. The development of strike aircraft has seen a reduction in the size of aircraft assigned to this role, and, although weapons-carrying capabilities have similarly been reduced, the effectiveness of bombing weapons, be they nuclear or conventional, has greatly improved.

In the UK, the only remaining V-bomber from the immediate postwar era is the Victor, now assigned to duties as an air-to-air refuelling tanker. France will be withdrawing its Mirage IV long-range bombers in the next few years and China (the PRC) retains only older-technology copies, slightly improved, of 1950s-vintage Soviet bombers.

The United States and the Soviet Union remain the only two powers who wish to follow on their classic bombers developed in the decade after the Second World War. The B-52 Stratofortress and the Tupolev series of aircraft remain in service (and will continue to do so, although in slightly revised roles). Their successors are the Rockwell B-1B and Northrop B-2A from the United States and the Tupolev Tu-26 'Backfire' and Tu-160 'Blackjack' from the Soviet Union.

Airborne Early Warning Originally conceived to provide carrier-based aircraft with 'over-the-horizon' radar cover, the airborne early warning (AEW) aircraft has grown in size and capability. While some AEW aircraft remain in Carrier Air Wings, the principal thrust in this role is land-based aircraft carrying a large airborne radar, able to detect targets on land, at sea and in the air. The Boeing E-3 Sentry remains paramount in this role, with similar aircraft being developed in the Soviet Union.

When talking of AEW today, radar reconnaissance is the principal tasking (other elements are discussed below), but the associated monitoring of enemy radio wavebands, to gain intelligence of enemy movements,

◄
Similar to the B-1B is the Soviet Union's Tupolev Tu-160 'Blackjack', seen here in company with a Norwegian F-16A of 331 Sqn. following its interception in international airspace. (RNorAF)

▼
The latest versions of the Boeing Sentry AWACS is the E-3D version being built for the RAF (illustrated) and the E-3F for France. Like the KC-135R, these are powered by CFM56 turbofans. (Boeing Defense & Space)

should not be ignored. Sigint (signals intelligence) is one area, while elint (electronic intelligence) is discussed under Electronic Warfare below.

Reconnaissance This subject covers a broad spectrum indeed, which boils down to discovering what the enemy is doing over the hill. Although satellite reconnaissance had now replaced the strategic air element (typified by the SR-71 'Blackbird' reconnaissance aircraft) at the top end, with human intelligence (i.e. spies) being at the other end, a place remains for tactical air reconnaissance. Neither satellite nor spy can guarantee immediate post-strike pictures of an air raid on some installation or formation of troops.

Traditionally, air reconnaissance has involved a camera-equipped aircraft (usually a derivative of a successful fighter or bomber) overflying an area, recording photographic images on 'wet' film. While the photographic camera remains with us, many reconnaissance systems are now going 'all-electric', in the form of

▶ Grumman's E-2 Hawkeye carrier-borne AEW aircraft has already been through several improvements and is currently receiving the APS-145 radar system. An Egyptian version of the aircraft is illustrated. The E-2 is making small-volume sales in areas where the E-3 Sentry is perceived as being too expensive a system. (Grumman)

infra-red imagery recorded on video tape. The resulting image shows more than the traditional photograph and can be transmitted, via a data link, to a ground station to provide almost 'real-time' data. Once on the ground, the air crew hand over a cassette to the intelligence community for interpretation. The ground support implicit in 'wet film' photographic reconnaissance is now being done away with, and reaction time is thereby much reduced.

While many of the recce platforms remain variants of in-service fighter or strike/attack aircraft, many other types can be used for such tasks simply by loading a suitable pod equipped with camera, FLIR (forward-looking infra-red) or SLAR (side-looking airborne radar) on to a weapons pylon. The US TARPS (Tactical Air Reconnaissance Pod System) is typical of such equipment. For short-range work, the remotely piloted vehicle (RPV) or unmanned air vehicle (UAV) has been developed and used with effect. Manned air reconnaissance is used more for deeper-penetration missions requiring immediate results.

Air-to-Air Refuelling Although developed before the Second World War, air-to-air refuelling (AAR) saw its greatest boost in the postwar establishment of the USAF's Strategic Air Command, when the capability was vital, enabling US bombers to reach their targets. However, the ability to refuel aircraft in flight was swiftly adopted for all types of tactical combat aircraft. Indeed, the UK's tanker force is deployed predominantly in support of the air defence force. However, strategic transport, AEW, maritime patrol and other tasks have also benefited from the advent of AAR. The haste with which RAF Nimrods and Hercules were fitted with an AAR capability during the Falklands conflict of 1982 is evidence of this flexibility – which was, at the time, referred to as a 'force expander'.

Although the USAF uses an American system of AAR, whereby the tanker has a 'flying' boom which is steered into a receptacle on the receiver aircraft by a boom operator on board the tanker, the rest of the world (the US Navy included) has adopted the 'probe and drogue' system, developed by Flight Refuelling in the UK. Here the tanker streams a pipe with a drogue at the tip, within which is a valve. The receiver aircraft is equipped with a probe which the pilot then places in the valve. The task has been described as attempting to pick up 'a doughnut on the end of a jousting lance'. Drogue systems can be installed in tanker aircraft or in pods; the latter can be fitted on virtually any type of aircraft with weapons pylons, enabling a 'buddy' system of refuelling to be conducted – for example, one fighter refuelling another.

Electronic Warfare In its widest sense, electronic warfare (or 'EW' as the acronymphomaniacs of MILSPEAK call it) refers to any electronic means used in warfare. However, in the context of air combat operations, it refers to both passive and defensive forms of electronic countermeasures (ECM), involving the detection and warning of hostile radar transmissions directed against the friendly aircraft, the use

▲
Destined to replace the C-141B in USAF service is the McDonnell Douglas C-17A airlifter. Studies are already under way to look at 'stretching' the aircraft and installing more powerful Rolls-Royce RB.211-535 turbofans in place of the current Pratt & Whitney F117. (LTV)

▶
Roughly equivalent to the US C-5 Galaxy is the Soviet Union's Antonov An-124 'Condor' (seen at Le Bourget in 1987)...

▶
...which has, itself, already been developed into the enlarged Antonov An-225 Myria, seen here at Farnborough in 1990. The fairings over the wing centre-section are to mount the Buran space shuttle vehicle, which the An-225 was specifically designed to transport. Note the extra pair of Lotarev D-18T turbofans. (Author)

of electronic jamming to disrupt the said radar signals and the deployment of chaff and flares to decoy such missiles as are launched against the friendly aircraft.

Dedicated aircraft fall into two basic categories. Escort or stand-off jammers carry a more complex ECM suite and are able to jam more frequencies than the average internal or pod-mounted ECM fit on combat aircraft. 'Wild Weasel' defence-suppression aircraft are fitted with special detection equipment, aimed at seeking out enemy SAM or AAA surveillance and tracking radar, and with anti-radar missiles (such as AGM-88 Harm or Alarm) which are then launched against these radars to neutralize these defences.

Strictly speaking, AEW, sigint and elint all come within the EW category; the first two have been covered already. Electronic intelligence is the gathering of enemy electronic data and transmissions of all types and its recording and deciphering, and the application of the knowledge gained in active ECM systems or dedicated EW aircraft. Elint aircraft are usually large multi-engined types, many being conversions of civil airliners.

Transport Air transport operations may involve either long-range strategic freight and troop deliveries (intra-theatre) or short-to-medium range tactical operations (inter-theatre), and both cover a wide variety of tasks. The range of air transport tasks includes airborne assault by parachute forces; air transport of formed units with all organic equipment; air supply operations, being the supply and maintenance of forces by either air-dropping or landing; aero-medical evacuation, in a chain, from the forward to rear base areas; and special airborne operations, designed for specific tasks, such as clandestine or *Spetznatz* operations. While intra-theatre operations are carried out by fixed-wing aircraft, most inter-theatre operations are carried out by helicopters, although some smaller air forces do maintain short-range fixed-wing STOL transports for some of these tasks. The helicopter aspects will be discussed in the next chapter.

Anti-Submarine Warfare (ASW) Maritime Strike (see below) and ASW are the two prime maritime operations. If one discounts helicopter ASW (discussed in the next chapter), then the prime fixed-wing ASW resource is the long-range patrol aircraft, equipped with a variety of sensors – including surface radar,

▲
The Lockheed P-3C Orion (illustrated here carrying Harpoon ASMs and Sidewinder AAMs) has been progressively developed over the years and, following the cancellation of its P-7 replacement, looks set to take on a new guise as the 'P-3½'. (Mark Meyer/US Navy)

FLIR, sonobuoys, magnetic anomaly detectors (MAD) and 'sniffers' to detect diesel fumes from a surfaced submarine – and with the weapons required to defeat submarines – depth charges, homing torpedoes and anti-ship missiles.

Typical of such aircraft is the P-3 Orion, operated by the US Navy. In some armed forces the navy takes the

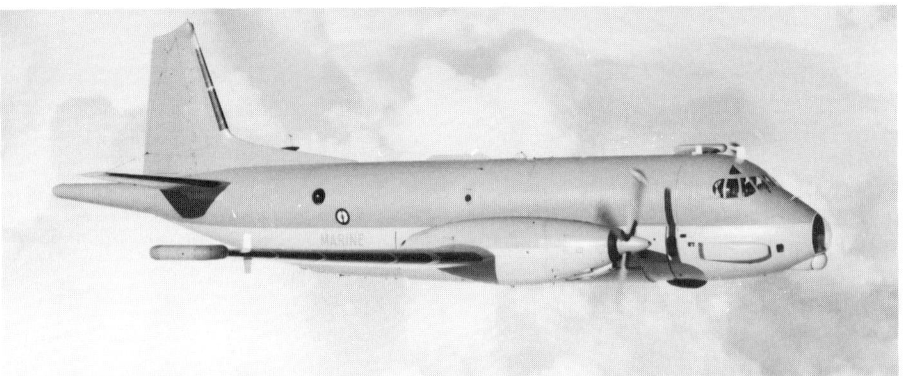

◄ The latest European maritime patroller is Dassault's Atlantique 2, with a production airframe and engines to the same original design (but with modern refinements) married to a new mission avionics system. (Dassault/Aviaplans)

lead in operating such aircraft and in others it is the air force. Some air arms possess only a limited ASW capability, in the form of slightly smaller or less sophisticated patrol aircraft whose job is purely surveillance or search-and-rescue (SAR). Indeed, in peacetime, many maritime patrol aircraft are deployed on such tasks.

Maritime Strike Sometimes known as anti-surface vessel warfare (ASuW), these operations are carried out by strike aircraft equipped with anti-ship missiles. They carry a radar system capable of detecting the enemy ships and designating the targets to the missiles. In some air arms, these missiles are part of the fit available to strike aircraft; in others they are operated in dedicated maritime strike units. Both air force and naval air units can be tasked with this role. Naval helicopter ASuW applications are considered in the next chapter.

Carrier Operations The task of an aircraft carrier is to project air power across the maritime environment and, as such, Carrier Air Wings are small-scale air forces in their own right, reflecting many of the roles already described. The US Navy is by far the largest exponent of carrier air power and the composition of one of its Air Wings is typical of the overall concept. It usually comprises two squadrons of fighter/air defence aircraft (F-14 Tomcat), dual role fighter/attack aircraft (F/A-18 Hornet), dedicated strike aircraft (A-6E Intruder, perhaps including some KA-6D Intruder tankers for carrier-based AAR), AEW (E-2C Hawkeye), ASW (S-2 Viking and/or SH-3G/H or SH-60F helicopter), and even transport (C-2 Greyhound, for carrier onboard delivery or COD). Such an Air Wing can number between 60 and 90 aircraft, depending on the exact nature of the carrier's deployment (e.g. strike-heavy or ASW-heavy) and on the size of the carrier itself. Less ambitious navies, limited by the cost of such forces, have adopted a mix of STOVL (Sea Harrier or AV-8A/B Harrier) aircraft plus helicopters to produce this mix of operational capabilities.

Aircraft with Potential

One could do a lot worse than consider those principal aircraft deployed in Operation 'Desert Storm' by way of examples of aircraft with potential to remain effective beyond this decade. They are in service today and many will, undoubtedly, still be in service beyond the turn of the century. With the basic platforms of air power remaining operational for well in excess of 25 years, it is the systems which are placed in the platforms which offer the most cost-effective means of keeping up to date with emerging threats.

Of the combat aircraft in service and deployed in the Gulf area, the most modern – the Lockheed F-117A 'Stealth' fighter – has been in service since 1983, work having begun in 1976. Its production run is complete (although there is talk of a second batch of B models) and a new generation of stealth fighters – the Lockheed F-22A 'Lightning II' – is only just beginning full-scale development.

Yet, strictly speaking, the F-117A fighter is not really a fighter in the traditional sense; rather it is a long-range, low-observable, tactical interdictor or strike aircraft. Today the term 'fighter' encompasses many of the roles which, previously, had dedicated types assigned them. 'Multi-role' is the trend in tasking and, as technology in all areas of military aviation has advanced,

▶
Derived from the RAF's Harrier GR.3, the Royal Navy's Sea Harrier is already being improved to FRS.2 standard. It is illustrated here carrying four AIM-120 AMRAAM missiles. (BAe)

these aircraft have become smaller and more effective. Aircraft half the size of the Lancaster and B-17 can deliver a larger bomb load to a more distant target. The General Dynamics F-111, Grumman A-6 Intruder, Saab AJ.37 Viggen, Panavia Tornado IDS, Sukhoi Su-24 'Fencer' and Mirage 2000S/N are typical strike aircraft of today. For the future, the successor to the A-6, the A-12 Avenger II stealth strike aircraft was being developed by General Dynamics and McDonnell Douglas for the US Navy, but following its cancellation in January 1991 more A-6s are to be re-winged and a new version of the Hornet, the F/A-18E/F is to be developed, pending a new A-12 replacement, the AX. Grumman has proposed an evolution of the F-14F, beginning with the F-14 Quickstrike, through the Super Tomcat 21 and the Attack Super Tomcat. The outcome of this procurement battle may not be resolved for some time.

What were once known as bombers are now, in the main, referred to as strike aircraft or strike fighters. The term 'bomber' now means a large aircraft capable of carrying and delivering conventional and nuclear weapons over long ranges. The Boeing B-52 Stratofortress remains the classic 'modern' bomber. Designed in the late 1940s, first flown in 1952 and entering service in 1955–56, the B-52 remains in service today and will still be in service at the turn of the century. The Rockwell B-1B and Tupolev Tu-22M/26 'Backfire' represent bombers of today, with the Northrop B-2 and Tupolev Tu-160 'Blackjack' representing tomorrow's advanced technology bombers.

The fighter, in the traditional sense, is now an air superiority fighter, usually with a secondary air-to-ground capability, able to destroy targets beyond visual range; or a (comparatively) lightweight air combat fighter with a more equally balanced role split between air-to-air tasks and air-to-ground tasks. The Grumman

▶
Seen here refuelling one of the two Lockheed YF-22A ATF prototypes is Boeing's latest Stratotanker, the KC-135R, re-engined with GE/SNECMA CFM56 turbofans. Already a further upgrade is under way which will incorporate a 'glass cockpit' and reduce the number of flight crew members by one. (Lockheed)

◀
The airborne arm of the French nuclear deterrent is being shared between the Mirage IVP and the Mirage 2000N; the latter is illustrated, armed with an ASMP cruise missile (just visible between the drop tanks). The 2000N was developed from the two-seat Mirage 2000B conversion trainer. Already a non-nuclear attack version, the Mirage 2000D, is under development for export. (SIRPA-Air)

▶▲
Looking to step into the F-4 Phantom's shoes is the McDonnell Douglas F/A-18 Hornet. Apart from the US Navy, it is in service with Australia (illustrated), Canada and Spain, under construction for Kuwait and selected by Switzerland. (Australian DoD)

◀
The Soviet equivalent to the USAF F-111 series is the Sukhoi Su-24 'Fencer', now being developed in a similar way to its US counterpart. (Flygvapnet)

◀
The export model of Dassault's Mirage 2000 currently under development in a multi-role version is the Mirage 2000-5, seen here with four MICA and two Magic 2 missiles. (Dassault/Aviaplans)

▶
The Saab JAS.39 Gripen is a true multi-role fighter and, despite troubled development, is set to become Sweden's main combat aircraft well into the next century. (Peter Liander/Saab)

F-14 Tomcat, McDonnell Douglas F-15 Eagle, Sukhoi Su-27 'Flanker', Panavia Tornado ADV, Saab JA.37 Viggen and Mirage 2000C are examples of the former, while the General Dynamics F-16, McDonnell Douglas F/A-18 Hornet, Saab JAS.39 Gripen, MiG-29 'Fulcrum', European Fighter Aircraft (as yet unnamed and known by its acronym EFA) and Dassault Rafale are examples of the latter. The way in which future technology will define the fighter is instanced by the two competitive prototypes for the USAF's ATF programme.

Midway between the fighter and the bomber came the fighter-bomber, usually a fighter type adapted to carry small bombs or rocket projectiles in support of ground forces in action. After 1945, these became known as fighter, ground-attack (or FGA) aircraft. Today the role has subdivided into close air support (formerly FGA) and attack – using shorter-range light bombers or strike aircraft. The Fairchild/Republic A-10 and the Harrier (in both the original British Aerospace AV-8A Harrier GR.1/3 or McDonnell Douglas/BAe AV-8B Harrier GR.5/7 form) and the Soviet Sukhoi Su-25 'Frogfoot' are examples of the former and the Aeritalia/Aermacchi/Embraer AMX typifies the current generation of the latter.

In the less glamorous but equally vital roles of maritime patrol and anti-submarine warfare (ASW), the Lockheed P-3 Orion, BAe Nimrod, Dassault-Breguet Atlantique and Tupolev Tu-154 'Badger' represent the current state of the art. Since the cancellation of the US Navy's successor to the Orion, the Lockheed P-7A, Dassault's Atlantique 2 (basically the airframe and engine combination of the original Atlantic with a current sensors and weapons suite) remains the only 'new' maritime patrol/ASW aircraft in production, although the US Navy still requires an Orion successor. This could well be a P-3C airframe with the T407 powerplant originally developed for the P-7.

Transport aircraft, too, have developed and their use is delineated between tactical and strategic roles. Lockheed have a virtual monopoly on such types in the West with the C-141 Starlifter and C-5 Galaxy on the strategic side and the ubiquitous C-130 Hercules on the tactical side (with strategic range when required). A new airlifter with tactical capability and strategic range, the McDonnell Douglas C-17 (as yet unnamed, but 'Dakota II' springs to mind) is under development in the United States. In the Soviet Union, Antonov have produced a whole range of transport types from the An-12 'Cub' (equivalent to the Hercules) to the An-124

◄
In a sense a cross between the F-16 and F/A-18, the Mikoyan MiG-29 'Fulcrum' has achieved several export sales and is already into a second (and possibly third) generation. It is seen here during the 1990 Farnborough Air Show carrying AA-10 (inboard) and twin AA-8 (outboard) missiles. (Author)

◄
Under development by four European nations – Germany, Italy, Spain and the UK – the European Fighter Aircraft is due to fly in 1992 and enter service in late 1996. (DASA)

►
The pre-production Dassault Rafale, C01 (not to be confused with the slightly larger Rafale-A), made its first flight in May 1991. Versions are being developed for the French Air Force and Navy, and export versions are very much in mind. (Dassault/Aviaplans)

◄
Under the consortium name Euroflag, five European manufacturers are to design and develop a replacement aircraft for the C-130 Hercules and Transall C-160, known at present as the Future Large Aircraft (FLA). (BAe)

'Condor' and its even larger brother the An-225 Myria (Dream), taking the records from the Galaxy. On the tactical side, the Ilyushin Il-76 'Candid' has replaced the 'Cub' and spawned several role-dedicated versions for air-to-air refuelling (AAR) and airborne early warning (AEW).

For the specialized role of AAR, conversions of bombers (in the 1960s/1970s) and commercial transports such as the Boeing 707 have been made. All three British V-bombers (Valiant, Vulcan and Victor) were converted to AAR tankers – the Victor remains in service – while the 707 produced the KC-135 and E-3 AWACS for AAR and AEW respectively. Even the McDonnell Douglas DC-10 provided the KC-10 Extender for the USAF and the Lockheed L.1011 TriStar and BAe VC.10 were converted to tanker/transports for the RAF. Export sales of the Boeing 707 configured for AAR have also been widely made.

Airborne early warning (AEW) and other forms of reconnaissance, visual and electronic, have also led to specialized aircraft, many of which will be with us in the twenty-first century. Typical are the Boeing E-3 Sentry AWACS (Airborne Warning and Control System) and its older but smaller brother, the Grumman E-2 Hawkeye. Even smaller systems, such as the heliborne Westland Sea King AEW.2A or the Pilatus Britten-Norman AEW Defender, have been developed. For surveillance, the infamous Lockheed U-2 was developed into the TR-1 and new aircraft built during the 1980s, although the Mach 3 Lockheed SR-71 'Blackbird' was withdrawn from service in mid-1990. For tactical reconnaissance work, modified in-service fighters, with either internal or pod-mounted equipment, are used.

If any trends are evident from the foregoing, it is that aircraft are becoming more flexible or multi-roled and that, in the case of combat aircraft, collaboration between companies and nations is becoming the norm. These aspects will be discussed in the forthcoming chapters.

The evolution of the helicopter since 1939 has seen rotary-wing technology applied to almost all the traditional fixed-wing combat roles, trading vertical performance for range and/or payload. Naval ASW is a major helicopter role today and for the future, as is heliborne attack (in several forms, but basically involving the anti-armour helicopter and the more general-purpose FGA gunship). The obvious advantage of vertical lift has also been applied to the transport role in all its forms, while the unique capability of the helicopter for saving lives in the search-and-rescue (SAR) role is daily demonstrated worldwide.

Yet the successor to the helicopter is already upon us – in the form of the tilt-rotor aircraft, epitomized by the Bell Boeing V-22 Osprey. It is still an endangered species on cost grounds (in the new era of declining defence budgets), but, at the time of writing, it is assured of development in the US FY92 defence budget (despite Pentagon attempts to cancel the programme) thanks to the experience of helicopter deployments during Operations 'Desert Shield' and 'Desert Storm' in the Middle East.

It is indicative of the value of the helicopter that it has come to be operated by all three arms of the forces, army, navy and air force alike. In some countries there is a blurring of responsibilities, and thus one sees the US Army operating all helicopters in support of land (but not Marine Corps) forces, while in the UK responsibility is split between the Army Air Corps and RAF. The latter situation has been 'in dispute' over many years, with some extremists suggesting that the Army fly the close support Harriers as well as all 'battlefield' helicopters. (However, the situation has been, for the time being, resolved at the status quo.)

Roles

Defence Suppression In a logical progression of defined roles for the armed helicopter, the first to be considered was the suppression of ground fire while deploying heliborne troops – resulting in the assault transport. The French were the first to mount machine guns, cannon and air-to-ground rocket projectiles on helicopters (the S-58/H-34 during operations in Algeria in the late 1950s) and the US forces followed with their UH-1Bs in Vietnam. The British Wessex (S-58/H-34) was equipped with machine guns and rockets during the Indonesian confrontation and beyond. Today, the UH-60A Black Hawks of the US Army continue the tradition with provision for door-mounted machine guns and the ability to carry, if required, Hellfire anti-tank guided weapons (ATGWs) on an external pylon.

From simple beginnings it was a short step to the fully dedicated 'gunship' used for escort and defence-suppression missions, but these were still derivatives of utility types with weapons mounted in the cabin, on small pylons or on the undercarriage skid assemblies. Again, the UH-1 Iroquois series, both B and D models, led the field – the armed 'Huey', as the Iroquois was

◄ The latest model in the army series of Westland Lynx helicopters is the AH.9, which features a wheeled undercarriage, derived from the Lynx 3, as well as other engine and system improvements. The British Army's 24th Air Mobile Brigade is to have sixteen of these helicopters but, unlike the AH.1/7 models, they will not be equipped with TOW missiles for the anti-tank role. (Westland)

HELICOPTERS WITH POTENTIAL

▶ The Kamov 'Hokum' helicopter is designed for air-to-air combat, although conversations during Le Bourget 1991 have led some western analysts to consider the 'Hokum' to have a naval rather than a land forces role. (US DoD/SMP-87)

affectionately known, becoming the 'Huey Cobra'. Its job was to saturate the landing zone with firepower before the assault helicopters landed their troops.

The need for a truly dedicated gunship helicopter led to Bell developing the AH-1G, christened the Cobra, from the dynamic components of the Iroquois. It was armed with a nose turret, which could carry a pair of 7.62mm mini-Gatling guns or a pair of 40mm grenade launchers or one of each, and fuselage-mounted stub wings, with two hardpoints each for the carriage of forward-firing gun or rocket pods. A tandem cockpit housed the pilot in the rear seat with the weapons operator (sometimes another pilot) in the front seat. There was no internal cabin for troops or cargo – it was the first true 'gunship' or, as the genre is known today, attack helicopter.

Anti-Armour In Vietnam, as the Vietcong began to use more sophisticated weaponry, including light armoured vehicles, the need to deploy ATGWs led to the installation to the BGM-71 TOW on the AH-1G. Although this system had only limited use, it was deemed successful in the role. With the end of the Vietnam War, the attack helicopter's future was assured and its anti-tank role was refined further for NATO missions in Europe (the AH-1S) as well as for naval use by the Marine Corps (with a twin-turbine P&WC T400 replacing the single Lycoming T53 engine) as the SeaCobra. The armed helicopter had arrived!

The anti-armour role is simply to deliver the most firepower against armoured forces as quickly and as accurately as possible, flying at low-level, using 'nap-of-the-earth' tactics to mask the helicopter from detection and ground fire. These assets are an organic part of Army formations, and their control is the ground commander's to exercise. Moreover, the response time is reduced, compared with fixed-wing CAS missions.

Anti-Helicopter The advent of armed helicopters has also prompted the need for non-offensive weapons to be installed on transport, cargo and reconnaissance types – the machine gun and cannon being standard fits these days. It was not a great step to take the man-portable SAM developments and offer an air-to-air version for helicopter use. The General Dynamics FIM-92 Stinger, Matra Mistral and Shorts Helistreak (derived from the Starstreak MANPADS) are typical examples. These developments have in turn led to the concept of the 'anti-helicopter helicopter', sometimes referred to as the 'fighter helicopter', and although the West has yet to deploy such a type operationally, according to the US DoD publication *Soviet Military Power* the Kamov Ka-136 'Hokum' helicopter is just such an animal. For the present, the West will, apparently, stick to offering self-defence AAMs as a standard fit on forthcoming armed helicopters.

Reconnaissance While there are many more sophisticated means of reconnaissance, the need for scouting the ground immediately to the front of the troop formations remains the job of the Army. The helicopter now assumes much of this recce role and the term 'scout' has now returned to the military vocabulary.

Airborne Assault The troop transport role was one of the early tasks assigned to the helicopter and one which has remained for tactical purposes. However, a more specialized aspect of this has been the deployment of troops into battle situations, whether or not the bullets are actually flying. Thus airborne assault has tended to become a part of the air mobility concept. In US parlance, troops thus deployed have become known as air cavalry and, in such a role, they are supported by armed helicopters of one description or another.

Airborne Re-supply This is the second major aspect of air mobility and, again, it has grown out of the original transport role. The supplying of equipment, ammunition and stores to military units on the ground or on board ships comes within this definition. When used in a naval context, re-supply at sea (RAS) or vertical replenishment (VERTREP) are terms which are used to describe what is essentially the same mission.

Aero-Medical Evacuation One of the first roles for any helicopter took advantage of its vertical capability

▲
Early versions of the US Army's Boeing CH-47 Chinook are being upgraded to a common, improved CH-47D standard, while a small number are being converted for special operations as the MH-47E. The RAF, one of the biggest overseas users of Chinooks, is having its fleet upgraded to CH-47D (Chinook HC.2) standard. (MoD/RAF)

◀
For use on ships unable to take Seahawks, the LAMPS Mk. I helicopter is the Kaman SH-2F. These are now being upgraded to SH-2G configuration with the GE T700 of the Seahawk. Illustrated is the development YSH-2G in the workshop. (Kaman)

►
Italy's A.129 Mangusta, from Agusta, was the first light attack helicopter in production and uses the Saab/Emerson Helitow system. (Agusta)

to save lives – extracting injured personnel from situations where fixed-wing aircraft were unable to operate. Most readers will be familiar with the pair of Bell 47 Sioux helicopters which fly in casualties for the opening sequence of the *M*A*S*H* television programme. Battle casualties were some of the first 'customers' and, today, 'aero-medical evacuation' is the term used to describe such operations, although the slightly older term 'casualty evacuation' (CASEVAC) is just as descriptive.

Special Operations The use of the helicopter to insert clandestine special or commando forces on covert missions is now covered by the term 'Special Operations'. While any transport helicopter could be used for such tasks, some air arms – notably the US Army and US Air Force – use specially modified helicopters with mission-specific equipment (such as terrain-following radars, FLIR sensors, additional armour protection and self-defence measures – guns and decoys) to conduct such operations.

Anti-Submarine Warfare (ASW) This role is exactly as one might expect – using the helicopter's special characteristics to deploy either detection systems, in the form of dipping (or 'dunking') sonar or sonobuoys, or weapons systems such as ASW torpedoes or depth charges, or both, from ships unable to deploy or launch fixed-wing aircraft against hostile submarines.

Anti-Surface Warfare (ASuW) Although the use of any gun- or rocket-armed helicopter against surface vessels implies an ASuW role, the latter is now assumed to involve a helicopter armed with anti-ship guided missile systems. Although such missiles are generally shorter in range than their larger land- or carrier-based brothers, the capability of the helicopter launch platform enables this range gap to be countered and even extended. This role may also be covered by the acronym ASV (anti-surface vessel).

Search-and-Rescue (SAR) Ever since their initial characteristic was proved and they were of sufficient size to carry more than two people, helicopters have been saving lives. Virtually any helicopter can be pressed into the SAR role but, like Special Operations helicopters, dedicated SAR 'birds' have mission-specialized equipment to enable them to conduct such operations. In peacetime, military helicopters tasked with the SAR role generally find their clientele to be civilian in nature. Specific military SAR tasks would include the 'planeguard' duties which always take place alongside an aircraft carrier during launch and recovery phases, or combat SAR, where specially configured helicopters are tasked with the recovery of downed aircrew in combat zones, often having to pick up the survivors in the face of hostile fire.

Helicopters with Potential

The versatility of the helicopter does not always allow one to allocate exact roles to specific types in this part of the text. Rather, an evolutionary approach must be adopted as military helicopters often find themselves performing complementary roles or even tasks which

◄
The latest anti-armour helicopter to fly, on 27 April 1991, is the Franco-German Tiger from Eurocopter (a joint venture between Aérospatiale and MBB/DASA). This will certainly be around for many years after its planned in-service date in the late 1990s. (Aérospatiale)

◄
Designed by Aérospatiale and marketed by Eurocopter, the SA.565 Panther multi-role helicopter is seen here in Brazilian Army markings. It can be armed with HOT anti-tank missiles or two 20mm gun pods or carry up to ten commandos. (Eucocopter)

◄
Although somewhat long in the tooth, the Soviet Union's Mil Mi-24 'Hind' (seen here in 'Hind-D' configuration at Redhill in 1990) has been progressively improved over several versions. (Richard Allen)

▶ The Soviet Union's 'Apache-lookalike' is the Mil Mi-28 'Havoc', unveiled to the West at Le Bourget in 1989. Note the heavy weapons load of rocket pods and AT-6 anti-tank missiles, and the 30mm chin-mounted cannon, plus nose sensors.

they would not normally be called upon to perform. If one considers the helicopters with potential in the order of roles described above, one immediately comes to the armed attack helicopter.

As the AH-1 series was developed, the US Army was already thinking of its second generation, the Advanced Attack Helicopter, and after a fly-off of two competing designs, the McDonnell Douglas Helicopter Company (MDHC; formerly Hughes Helicopters) AH-64 Apache was selected. The experience of the AH-1 Cobra was much in evidence but so too was the need for a dedicated, fully survivable system which could kill tanks in all weathers and at night. The first Apaches entered US Army service in July 1986 and over 600 of the 807 ordered have been delivered. As with all current in-service aircraft, the manufacturers have been working towards improving their product, in close collaboration with the US Army. In August 1989 MDHC received a design and development contract to provide four prototype AH-64B Longbow Apaches, with a view to upgrading at least 220 A models to this configuration from 1993 in a multi-stage improvement programme (MSIP). The name 'Longbow' comes from the Martin Marietta/Westinghouse Longbow millimetric-wave fire control radar, formerly known as the Airborne Adverse Weather Weapon System (AAWWS), which will be mast-mounted on the AH-64.

Italy's Agusta A.129, developed from the company's A.109 utility helicopter in much the same way as the Huey Cobra evolved, is the only other dedicated anti-armour helicopter now in production, with 60 on order for the Italian Army. Although an improved version was proposed under a four-nation development known as Tonal, this has now been abandoned. However, development of the existing A.129 with, for example, new engines (the LHTEC T800 turboshaft) is likely to be seen, probably more with a view to the export market than the domestic one.

Now under full-scale development is the Franco-German Tiger (once known as the Common Anti-Tank Helicopter, CATH) being developed by Eurocopter (Aérospatiale and MBB/Deutsche Aerospace) to fulfil the French Army's HAP/HAC and the German Army's PAH-2 requirements. The programme almost foundered in 1986 as costs rose for the separate development of three versions, but by March 1987 a compromise was re-launched. This involved the development of a basic airframe from which the CATH (HAC/PAH-2) versions and a separate escort HAP were derived. Like all contemporary attack helicopters, the Tiger will feature many survivability features. These include infra-red suppressors and armour for the engines; ballistic-tolerant rotor blades and hub; crash-worthy, armoured seats; crashworthy and self-sealing fuel tanks; a crushable bottom structure; energy-absorbing landing gear; and a low radar signature, incorporating an anti-radar treatment for the canopy windshields.

As with many Western military concepts, the Soviet Union has worked on parallel lines and, from the Mi-8 'Hip' transport helicopter, the Mil bureau developed the Mi-24 'Hind' gunship, first revealed in 1974. It did, however, retain an internal cabin. The current Mil Mi-28 'Havoc', however, is very much a dedicated anti-armour helicopter without any internal accommodation (apart from that for the two-man crew). It made its début in the West at Le Bourget in 1989 and its similarity to the Apache did not cause surprise.

◀
Based on the JetRanger/OH-58 Kiowa series, Bell's 406CS Combat Scout is the latest version in a series of military developments. This is the first 406CS for the Saudi Arabian Army. (Bell)

The latest attack helicopter to be unveiled is the South African CSH-2 Rooivalk, built by the Armscor subsidiary Atlas Aircraft. It has been developed to an SAAF requirement, and it is understood that component systems of the Rooivalk were tested during operations in Angola in 1987, prior to the first flight in February 1990. However, since the South Africans' withdrawal from Namibia, the official requirement has lapsed, although Armscor have continued with flight testing with a view to the export market.

Of course, not every nation can afford the luxury of dedicated attack helicopters, and several light and medium utility types have been adapted as multi-role armed helicopters. Types such as the Aérospatiale AS.565 Panther and the Sikorsky H-76 Eagle do not pretend to be as complex as their dedicated 'big brothers' but they do offer flexibility, wherein observation, reconnaissance and target designation may be combined with escort, fire-suppression and the movement of troops or small ground-based ATGW teams into ambush positions.

Placed midway between the multi-role armed helicopter and the dedicated attack helicopter are the anti-armour helicopters which carry a dedicated warload of ATGWs and their associated fire control systems yet which are not true attack helicopters. In Europe, several nations have adapted standard utility or observation types to carry either the Hughes TOW or Euromissile HOT missiles. Such systems are seen as a rapid counter to an enemy armoured breakthrough, bringing concentrated anti-armour firepower to bear where it is needed swiftly. They are also considered no more than a first generation. The British Army's Westland Lynx AH.1/7, the French Aérospatiale SA.342 Gazelle and AS.555 Fennec, the Agusta A.109 from Italy and the MBB Bo.105CB/P (PAH-1) in service with Sweden and Germany are typical examples. Others include the MD500/530 Defender range and Bell 406

◀
First flown in February 1990, South Africa's CSH-2 Rooivalk was designed for an SAAF requirement in Namibia which disappeared shortly before its first flight. The state company Armscor continues development, through its Atlas subsidiary, in the hopes of exporting the Rooivalk and is looking for an international partner to share development costs. (Armscor)

Combat Scout from the United States and Romania's IAR-317 Airfox, derived from the Alouette III and built under licence. Such armed helicopters represent an acknowledgement of the requirement for a dedicated anti-armour helicopter but with the need to acquire this capability at minimum cost by using existing airframes rather than specialist ones.

The one exception to the rule in this category is the US Army's Light Helicopter (LH, formerly LHX) programme. Initiated as a successor to the US Army's 2,000 OH-58 and OH-6 helicopters, as well as to some 1,000 AH-1S Cobras, this scout/attack helicopter has come under some heavy scrutiny in the United States. Yet the US Army has placed a high priority on this programme. Two industry teams were bidding for this vital contract: Boeing/Sikorsky (the 'First Team') and Bell/MDHC (the 'Super Team'). Both teams cited wide experience in designing their solutions to the requirement, with the 'First Team' solution incorporating a 'Fantail' fenestron-like, anti-torque rotor and the 'Super Team' adopting the NOTAR (no tail rotor) approach. Both teams submitted their final proposals on 1 September 1990 and the US Army's decision, in favour of the Boeing/Sikorsky design, was announced on 5 April 1991.

The powerplant of the RAH-66A Comanche, as the LH is now officially designated, will be the LHTEC (a teaming of Allison and Garrett) T800-LHT-800 turboshaft engine of 1,300shp. The avionics Mission Equipment Package (MEP) is designed to give the RAH-66A a full day/night/adverse weather capability and much development and testing has already been carried out on the systems. The armament is fixed at a maximum of eight Hellfire ATGWs and four Stinger air-to-air missiles (AAMs), plus a 20mm Gatling-type cannon. Stealth technology was incorporated in both the rival designs. With a 'go-to-war' empty weight no more than 3,400kg, a cruise speed of 170kts and a self-ferry deployment range of 1,260nm (2,300km), the RAH-66A looks to be an attractive solution to a number of US Army procurement problems. In common with all current US military projects, however, the greatest threat to its continued development is its high cost. At the time of the selections, a US Army official joked that the LH programme 'was the whale that swallowed the Army procurement budget'. In order to slow down the rate of expenditure and reduce the overall programme costs, the US Secretary of Defense, Richard Cheney, announced in September 1990 that the whole programme would be extended by two years with the addition of a prototype phase. In addition, he announced that the US Army's goal of a 2,096-strong LH fleet would be reduced to one of 1,292. The first prototype RAH-66A is scheduled to make its maiden flight in November 1993. The demonstration/validation (dem/val) prototyping phase is expected to run until October 1994, when full-scale development (FSD) should begin. Initial low-rate production begins in November 1996, and the delivery of the first production Comanche is scheduled for December 1997. Many of

► Aérospatiale's SA.332 Super Puma has won many orders around the world as it has been progressively developed. Illustrated is a troop transport version for the Spanish Army. (Aérospatiale)

the lighter helicopters already mentioned were originally developed for the recce or scout roles and, suitably updated, will see service well into the twenty-first century. Of these types, the US RAH-66A Comanche programme is the only 'new' helicopter in this category.

Moving on to the transport helicopter, with its various refined role configurations, the Sikorsky S-70/UH-60 series Black Hawk will continue in service as a medium-sized utility type for many years to come. Equivalent helicopters would include the Lynx, SA.330 Puma and AS.532 Cougar (Super Puma), variants of the Bell 212/412 (UH-1N), the utility version of the Anglo-Italian EH.101 and the Soviet Union's Mi-8/17 'Hip' series. In the heavy-lift category, the Boeing CH-47 Chinook series and Sikorsky's CH-53E Super Stallion represent the largest helicopters in the West, and the Mil Mi-26 'Halo' is the Soviet Union's equivalent. The United States is currently developing Special Operations variants of the H-60 Black Hawk and H-47 Chinook in a parallel programme, using a common avionics suite.

On the naval side, there are two basic types of heli-

▲
Sikorsky's S-70 Black Hawk utility transport helicopter has been adapted for many roles. Illustrated here is the latest UH-60L in US Army service, carrying an M988-series Hummer light vehicle. (Sikorsky)

►
The Soviet Union's Mil Mi-26 'Halo' is one of the biggest helicopters in both military and civil service. Its payload could comprise up to 85 combat-equipped troops or two airborne infantry combat vehicles. (Author)

◄
The Seahawk was adopted as a replacement for the SH-3H Sea King in US Navy service as the SH-60F 'CV-helo'. Its new suite of mission avionics includes a dipping sonar. (Sikorsky)

►
The US Coast Guard, too, saw the advantages of the S-70 series, and the HH-60J Jayhawk is a medium-range rescue helicopter, capable of flying out to a 300nm radius and rescuing six survivors. The US Navy operates a basically similar variant, the HH-60H, as a combat SAR helicopter. (Sikorsky)

copter in use, covering the roles already described, which can be expected to continue in service into the next century. The smaller helicopter, for ASW and ASuW, is represented by the naval variant of the Lynx and its developments, the SH-60 Seahawk and its developments, the SH-2 Seasprite and the AS.565F Dauphin 2. The latest small-ship helicopter is the four-nation NH-90 naval variant being developed by France, Germany, Italy and the Netherlands. The larger naval helicopter has for the past 25 years been represented by the Sikorsky Sea King and its variants (built under licence by Italy, Japan and the UK), used for ASW and in some other specialized roles. With over 1,000 built, the Sea King will certainly be around into the next century. However, the Anglo-Italian EH.101 Merlin was designed as a Sea King replacement and, initially, has been selected by Canada, Italy and the UK. Once the Merlin is in service, it is probable that many Sea King operators will consider it as a replacement for their Sea Kings.

As explained earlier, virtually any helicopter type in service in other roles (apart from dedicated attack heli-

►
The Black Hawk was adopted by the US Navy as its Light Airborne Multi-Purpose System (LAMPS) Mk. III for use on 'small ships' as the SH-60B Seahawk. An example is shown here landing on the deck of the USS *McInerney*. Note the nose ESM sensors, radar and, near the tail, MAD 'bird'. (Sikorsky)

▲
The Lynx HAS.8 is being equipped with a new Central Tactical System (CTS), a nose-mounted Passive Identification Device (PID) and a new MAD system. This photograph shows an interim HAS.8 with the CTS and PID fitted. (HMS *Osprey*)

►
The naval version of the Eurocopter Dauphin, the SA.565F, distinguished itself during the Gulf War in Saudi Navy service by destroying a number of Iraqi naval vessels with its Aérospatiale AS.15TT missiles. This photograph shows a test-firing of the AS.15TT during pre-delivery trials. (Aérospatiale)

►
Seen here in mock-up form is the new NATO Helicopter for the 1990s (NH-90) in its naval version with a Murene lightweight torpedo and an AM.39 Exocet anti-ship missile. It is being developed jointly by Aérospatiale of France, Agusta of Italy, MBB/DASA of Germany and Fokker of the Netherlands. (Aérospatiale)

◀ Derived from the Kamov Ka-27 'Helix-A' ASW helicopter, the Ka-27PS 'Helix-D' model is equipped with extra fuel tanks and a winch above the port-side door, for planeguard SAR duties on board the new class of Soviet aircraft carriers. (TASS)

▶ Derived from the Sikorsky S-61/SH-3 series, Westland's Sea King HAS.5 is seen here about to dunk its sonar. Versions have been adopted as AEW platforms, as assault helicopters, as maritime attack helicopters and for SAR duties. (Racal/RN)

copters) can be adapted for SAR work. Thus any of the major types mentioned above can be seen fulfilling this role. Specifically, the Lynx, Dauphin, Alouette III, H-60 series and Sea King can all be found in specialized SAR configurations. For the future, it is known that Canada is looking at an SAR derivative of the EH.101 and, eventually, if previous UK procurement patterns are followed, the EH.101 will enter both RN and RAF service as dedicated SAR aircraft.

By far the greatest potential for developing the helicopter comes in the form of the TiltRotor craft, exemplified by the Bell XV-15 research vehicle and the Bell Boeing V-22 Osprey mentioned earlier. Described, varyingly, as a turboprop aircraft with vertical take-off

▶ The Sea King's replacement in both the Italian and Royal Navies will be the EH Industries EH.101, built jointly by Agusta of Italy and Westland. The RN version (illustrated) is named Merlin HAS.1 and last year the UK MoD announced that the IBM Federal Systems/Westland consortium had been appointed as prime contractor for the complete Merlin system. (API)

◀
A version of the CH-53E Super Stallion, Sikorsky's MH-53E Sea Dragon is one of the very few helicopters dedicated to airborne mine countermeasures (AMCM) using special towed sleds. These helicopters were used to effect during the latter part of the Gulf War, clearing sea lanes of the Iraqi mine barrage. (Sikorsky)

and landing (VTOL) capability or a helicopter which can adapt to an aircraft mode for a faster transit speed, the TiltRotor is 'neither fish nor flesh'. Early trials have proved the efficacy of the concept but its high acquisition cost has forced the Pentagon to cancel the programme. However, pressure from both sides of the US Congress has ensured that funds continue to be spent on the programme: three Production Representative Aircraft were due to be authorized under FY92. The 'driver' of the V-22 is the US Marine Corps and, despite being part of the Navy (for funding purposes), the Corps has a reputation for getting exactly what it wants in order to perform its mission. Its acquisition of the Harrier STOVL close-support fighter, off-the-shelf from the UK, is a case in point. Although Marine and political opinion is in favour of the V-22, it must be said that the Osprey is still an endangered species.

Summarizing, it can be said that the helicopters that will be seen around well into the next century are those which we can see flying today – even the V-22, we hope. Only the RAH-66A and NH-90 remain to be flown at the time of writing ...

◀
A collaborative venture between Bell and Boeing to introduce a new class of rotorcraft known as the TiltRotor resulted in the V-22 Osprey. Although revolutionary, the V-22 is finding it hard to reach production status owing to US DoD budget restraints. (Boeing)

LOW OBSERVABLES AND STEALTH AIRCRAFT

If it is accepted that before attempting to neutralize air power it must first be detected, whether from the ground or from another aircraft, then it follows that the best way of applying air power with success is to make aircraft less visible to the enemy. This, in a nutshell, is what 'stealth' technology is all about. Another term for this concept, presently in vogue in the United States, is 'low observability'. However, someone coined the word 'stealth' and the media adopted it, so 'stealth' it has become.

However, before delving into the basics of what is highly classified technology, it must be pointed out that stealth is not a quality that can be given by just adding a 'black box' to an aircraft or giving it a coat of special 'anti-radar' paint. The Klingon 'Cloaking Device' of *Star Trek* fame does not yet exist. Stealth is the application of many and varied technologies to an aircraft and its operational equipment. Indeed, it is possible to retrofit some stealth technology to aircraft designed and built before the concept was refined.

It must also be stated that stealth or low-observability technology is not new: it is, perhaps, better known as camouflage, and it dates back to the First World War. Up until the end of the Second World War, camouflage paint schemes were only a means of reducing the visual signature of an aircraft (or ship or armoured fighting vehicle). However, the advent of radar began to change the interpretation of the concept. It still concerns itself with the reduction of visual signatures, but it now takes in the confusion of other sensors available to combat aircraft and ground-based air defence systems.

The first attempt at this was 'Window' – brown paper coated with metallic paint and cut to length to match enemy radar wavebands. Used from 1944 and dropped by Allied night bombers, it was intended to 'spoof' enemy radars into thinking that there were vast formations of aircraft where they were, in reality, just a handful. From such simple but effective origins began the art that is today known as electronic warfare or EW.

The aerospace industry has been capable of producing aircraft with features to reduce an aircraft's acquisition by surveillance radars and other sensors for some years. The first stealth aircraft now lies in a dusty hangar belonging to the Smithsonian Institute at Silver Hill, Maryland. It is the third prototype of the Horten Ho 9 flying wing, built in Germany in 1944–45. It used plywood and a very early form of radar absorbent material (RAM) in its construction, in order not to present a radar reflective surface, while the engines were buried beneath this RAM in the centre of the fuselage. What is new about stealth is the integration of various methods of confusion and signature-reduction into one airframe to ensure that the whole is, apparently, less than the sum of its parts – to an enemy sensor system at least. The longer a combat aircraft remains undetected, the better the chance it has of achieving its mission and returning to base – the ultimate in designing for survival.

Since the initiation of what are now referred to as 'Black' projects in the United States in 1980, low-observable technologies could not be written about in great technical depth in non-classified publications. While the aerospace industry and its commentators had, for several years, been talking about a stealth fighter in service with the USAF, on 10 November 1988 the USAF finally revealed the existence of the Lockheed F-117A and published one photograph. The reason given for 'going public' on the existence of the F-117A was the need to expand the aircraft's operational applications to daylight hours. It might also be added that much of its technology was about to be overshadowed by the roll-out of the B-2. No funding details were revealed and there are criticisms of cost overruns.

So, to appreciate what stealth is all about, who better to describe it than Ben Rich. Before his recent retirement, he was successor to the late Clarence 'Kelly' Johnson as President of Lockheed's Advanced Development Company in Burbank, California – otherwise known as the 'Skunk Works', where the U-2, SR-71 and F-117A were conceived and built. Speaking with the author during the Farnborough Air Show in September 1990, Rich explained the basic principles of stealth, which he described as his 'six disciplines of low observability' – the design criteria which must be traded off, one against the other, to ensure optimum overall compatibility. These he lists as 'radar cross-section, infrared, smoke, contrail, visibility and noise. You've got to balance all these,' he said.

In balancing these criteria, the basic role requirements of the aircraft must be taken into account. As always there will be a compromise, but one that pushes technological breakthroughs. 'Once we get a technological breakthrough,' says Rich, 'we've got to keep using it.' Referring to the Lockheed developments in the field of stealth aircraft (the 'Have Blue' projects), and the company's success in manufacturing the first production stealth fighter for the USAF, Rich main-

tains that 'we've given the military a new dimension and now they have to learn how to use that new dimension'. This, the USAF has been out and done – first in Operation 'Just Cause' in December 1989 over Panama and more recently during Operation 'Desert Storm' over Iraq and Kuwait.

To appreciate and, it is hoped, explain the mysteries of stealth aircraft and the application of low observables, the four major US programmes will now be examined. They must be US programmes as no other nation is releasing details of stealth projects – if, indeed, any other equivalent projects are being undertaken. These are, in effect, the new shapes in the sky into the twenty-first century. The addition of stealth to existing airframes currently in service or under development will also be referred to and illustrated as appropriate.

Stealth Fighter

First flown in June 1981, the F-117A has been operational with the 440th Tactical Group at Nellis AFB, Nevada, since October 1983, flying from the Tonopah Test Range airfield, also in Nevada. A total of 59 aircraft have been delivered. The F-117A is what is known today as a tactical fighter or interdictor and it is able to carry 'the full range of USAF tactical fighter ordnance'. This includes one 2,000lb BLU-109 Paveway II low-level laser-guided bomb or the AGM-65 Maverick air-to-surface missile. The external carriage of weapons, fuel tanks or other stores on pylons under the wings and fuselage greatly increases the radar cross-section, and obviously would detract from the F-117A's stealth capability, so munitions, etc., are accommodated in an internal weapons bay behind and beneath the single-pilot cockpit.

Limiting the space for internal weapons carriage helped to keep the physical size of the aircraft small. Like the De Havilland Mosquito Mk. II light bomber of the Second World War, it has no defensive armament (i.e. guns) with which to deter attackers. The Mosquito relied on its speed to escape interception (although it also had certain stealth characteristics in that it was of purely wooden construction, thereby reducing its radar reflectivity). The F-117A relies totally on its stealth features to avoid, or drastically reduce the chance of, detection rather than on its speed, as it is an operationally subsonic aircraft.

In appearance, the F-117A resembles a multi-faceted pyramid, whose apex is behind the cockpit, with a wing sweep angle of 67 degrees. The decision to adopt the 'flat-plane' concept was taken to enable the aircraft to deflect radar signals – specifically those from airborne early warning (AEW) aircraft flying above it and looking down. The radar energy is deflected away at various angles and thus generates a weaker return to the AEW radar, reducing the radar cross-section. The use of flat, vertical surfaces on the F-117A, while complying with known low-radar-return techniques, is opposite in technique to that of the blended, smooth contours of the Northrop B-2: the use of such smooth, flat surfaces with distinct edges reduces radar backscatter. Composite materials, with known radar absorbent capabilities in addition to their 'strength for less weight' features, also help to reduce the radar cross-section, which can be further assisted by the use of matt 'iron-ball' paint in black or midnight blue, offering extra radar absorption with a reduced visual signature at night.

The use of a 'vee-tail' configuration, with an opposing angle of 85 degrees, suggests that both leading and trailing edges of the sharply swept 'ruddervators' have control surfaces. The trailing edge of the wings appear to have conventional control surfaces. The quadruple-redundant fly-by-wire control system includes a powerful stability augmentation system on the aircraft. The F-117A would appear to be inherently unstable and requires such systems for effective control. Should one channel fail, the remainder remain operational; if a second channel fails, it flies on two. Some early aircraft are thought to have experienced problems in this area. Since entering service, three F-117As are known to have crashed. A Lockheed test pilot safely ejected from the first crash, which the USAF declines to date. The second crash occurred during the night of 11 July 1986 at Bakersfield, California, and the third on 14 October 1987 over the Nellis AFB ranges. Both USAF pilots involved in these accidents were killed. This problem has been addressed and safety has now improved.

The powerplant of the F-117A comprises a pair of General Electric F404-GE-F1D2 turbofan engines, derived from those used on the F/A-18 Hornet but tuned for subsonic performance. The use of non-afterburning, turbofan engines reduces noise and smoke. Burying the engines in the fuselage centre also reduces

◄▲ The Lockheed F-117A stealth fighter was first flown in 1981, but its combat début in December over Panama was not exactly conspicuous. Its performance during the Gulf War, however, proved the effectiveness of the aircraft and of its low-observable features. (Lockheed)

► The angular form of the F-117A can be seen here in the static park at Le Bourget in 1991. Three of the four air-data sensors (pitot tubes) can be seen on the flat leading edge of the nose, while the ball-shaped device above the 'nose cone' is a FLIR turret. Both the FLIR turret fairing and the engine air intakes are covered by a fine mesh to improve the low observability of the aircraft. (Author)

► This rear view of the F-117A (again at Le Bourget 1991) shows the wide but narrow engine exhausts of the aircraft and the large trailing-edge control surfaces. The apparent 'notch' in the starboard fin is caused by the all-moving ruddervator being slightly out of alignment. (Author)

the chance of radar reflection from the engine fans, especially where the front of the engine is close to a large, open air intake. The need for long, complex air inlet systems, however, puts pressure on the internal structure and overall size of the aircraft. The shrouded intakes are almost square, while the efflux is exhausted over the trailing edge of the rear fuselage in 'platypus' nozzles, protected by a heat shield of tiles similar to those used on the Space Shuttle. Auxiliary inlets, on the horizontal surfaces to the rear of the intakes, allow cold external air to bypass the engine to mix with the exhaust gases for cooling. Both these measures reduce the infra-red signature of the aircraft.

The cockpit glazing is of the windscreen/side windows type in five angular sections. Provision for boom-and-socket aerial refuelling is made on the upper fuselage decking aft of the cockpit. What was originally thought to be the refuelling socket, visible ahead of the windscreen, is now known to be a recessed FLIR sensor, covered by a fine mesh screen. A further FLIR sensor and laser designator are housed in a retractable turret beneath the forward fuselage. The four 'spikes' at the nose are air data sensors for airspeed and altitude sensing. The F-117A is not fitted with a radar of any description and so navigation is conducted by means of a high-precision inertial navigation system (INS) coupled to a Global Positioning System (GPS)/Navstar integrated into a digital nav/attack system, with automated mission planning facilities. The pilot is known to be able to use night-vision goggles.

The performance of the F-117A during Operation 'Desert Storm' gave the USAF its first real opportunity to assess the effectiveness of stealth in action; the Panama operation was, in effect, nothing more than a low-key operational trial. Over 45 F-117As were deployed in action during the Gulf War and proved most effective. All their missions were deemed successful and no aircraft were lost to enemy fire. Yet that alone does not mean that there is no room for improvement. Already the USAF is talking about a second production batch (Lockheed built 59 examples of the A model, the last being delivered in 1990), and there was talk of the RAF acquiring a number.

Stealth Bomber

Unlike the Stealth Fighter, which was never officially admitted to exist until November 1988, the existence of the Northrop B-2 Advanced Technology Bomber (ATB) has never been denied. When, in October 1981, President Reagan announced the decision to procure 100 B-1B bombers, it was also announced that another highly survivable strategic penetration bomber, with even lower observables than the B-1B, would be developed. The declared requirement was for 132 ATBs, 120 of which would be nuclear-capable. Since then, however, the Cold War has thawed and the lessons of the Gulf War are being absorbed. The US FY1991 budget reduced the requirement of B-2As down to 75 aircraft. There is no doubt that the B-2 has become a 'political' aeroplane and, at the time of writing, only fifteen have been funded.

Not surprisingly, information regarding the aircraft was non-existent, although commentators were predicting that the basic design would be of the 'flying wing' type. Northrop had, immediately following the Second World War, worked on such a configuration, flying a twin-engined, scaled-down version, the N-9M. The full-scale design, the XB-35, was a piston-engined heavy bomber and three of the fourteen ordered were later converted to YB-49 eight-jet and YRB-49A six-jet configuration. A production order for 30 B-49s was cancelled in 1949. Speculation on the exact configuration of the expected flying wing design was just as rife as with the Stealth Fighter. It came as a complete surprise when, on 20 April 1988, the USAF released an artist's impression of the B-2. The author, writing in the June 1988 issue of the journal *Defence*, commented: 'As might be expected ... [the impression] is heavily sanitised'. The then USAF Chief of Staff, General Larry D. Welch, told the media that 'there are a few details that are obscured for security reasons'. He also told reporters at the time, 'Everything you see there in that representation, if it's there, it's right.'

The General was right. At the official roll-out of the B-2A on 22 November 1988, the aircraft was as depicted in the USAF artist's impression. Like the Horton design, it is of flying wing configuration, with smooth, blended contours. The B-2A meets all the basic requirements of providing a reduced radar cross-section, being free of fins and vertical fuselage sides, while the engines, perforce, were buried in the centre of the wing. That said, the reason for the adoption of the flying wing concept was, on the Horten Ho 9, mainly to reduce drag on the airframe, with all fuel and weapons to be carried internally, rather than for what today we call stealth characteristics.

▶ The first Advanced Technology bomber, the Northrop B-2A, made its maden flight on 23 September 1989. Unlike the F-117A, the B-2A has smooth blended curves. Following the Gulf War, the USAF is stressing the conventional bombing role as well as the nuclear deterrent value of the B-2, of which it needs a minimum of 75 aircraft. (Northrop/US DoD)

Northrop took the Horten concept a stage further in the late 1940s when the company developed its XB-35 flying wing bomber. However, its conventional airscrews neutralized much of the advantage offered by its reduced radar cross-section. This conundrum was resolved with the jet-powered derivative, the YB-49, which demonstrated significant reductions in radar cross-section in trials against US coastal radar stations in 1948.

As noted above, the production B-49s were cancelled. The reason was that the aircraft could not meet USAF requirements in control and stability. It took too long for the pilot to level out for the bombing run. This is not really surprising, considering the technology of the time. With a conventional aircraft, changes can be made to the vertical control surfaces to respond to problems encountered in the control/stability region. With a flying wing – even allowing for the B-49's small fixed fins – the flying characteristics are different and a change in one axis of flight tends to affect the other two. To overcome such problems the tail surfaces are usually 'tweaked' – the YB-49 did have first-generation power-boosted flight controls and an early stability augmentation system (SAS) which detected and automatically corrected motion in the yaw axis. What it needed was modern, lightweight, computer-controlled systems, and the electronics technology of the 1940s would have to wait for another 40 years before miniaturization came along.

There were other reasons behind the decision to suspend the development of the flying wing. While the concept was right, the technology was not there to enable it to be effective in the supersonic bomber mission that the US Strategic Air Command was pushing in the late 1940s and early 1950s. As it was, these supersonic bomber projects resulted in two production designs – the Convair B-58 Hustler followed by the General Dynamics FB-111A – complementing the B-47 Stratojet and B-52 Stratofortress. The B-52 is with us today and is likely to remain on the USAF inventory through the first decade of the next century.

If one discounts the North American XB-70 Valkyrie, of which only two were built before cancellation, the first real replacement for the B-52 was the Rockwell B-1A. While not a stealth aircraft in today's sense, it does have a much lower radar cross-section than the BUFF (Big Ugly Fat Fella), as the B-52 is affectionately known. Work was begun on the B-1A in 1969 and progressed to prototype flying until President Jimmy Carter cancelled the project in 1977. Developmental flying was to continue with the three prototypes and one pre-production aircraft until, with a change of administration, President Ronald Reagan announced his decision to procure 100 B-1Bs in 1981. At this stage the experience of developmental flying and also advances in technology enabled the B-1B version to become more stealthy. By refining and modifying a small number of areas of the design, such as the engine intakes, the cockpit region and the aircraft's radar antennae, the B-1B's radar cross-section was reduced by 90 per cent compared with that of the B-1A.

At the same time as the B-1B was ordered into production, Northrop swung into action on the B-2A. The FSD contract was let a month after the Reagan announcement, Northrop appointing Boeing Advanced Systems and LTV's Aircraft Product Group as sub-contractors, with General Electric providing the engines. In November 1987 Northrop was awarded a $2 billion contract for B-2 production, with a view to attaining an initial operating capability by the early 1990s.

The B-2A is far from being a new-technology YB-49. Northrop has gone back to the drawing board, absorbed all the lessons of 40 years' advancement of technology in materials, aerodynamics, flight control systems, navigation, radar and engines, and come up with a new interpretation. The most outstanding feature is the way the trailing edge is shaped. The outer wings are almost conventional, but the trailing edge is 'double-W' shaped, with the engines exhausting through the two cut-ins of the centre 'W'. The domed centre-section houses the two crewmen (with provision for a third seat), avionics and weapons bays. On either side are the engine domes with scalloped edges to the air intakes. The depth of the centre-section is more

◀
The genesis of the B-2A from the Northrop 'flying wings' of the 1950s is apparent in this view of the aircraft. Note the buried engine exhausts set back into the engine pod fairings and the various control surfaces on the wing trailing edge. (LTV/Northrop)

▼
The smooth appearance of the B-2A is seen in this photograph of the aircraft taking off. Note the notched contours of the nosegear door and the large main undercarriage doors. (Rockwell)

than was expected and, to quote Bill Sweetman, 'it resembles a manta ray in an advanced stage of pregnancy'.

Like any modern combat aircraft, the B-2A is naturally unstable. However, unlike the YB-49, the B-2A has the advantages of a modern General Electric digital flight control system which, like that of the F-117A, is quadruplex in character. The control inputs from the pilot are transferred into electronic signals and, when these signals are directed to the central computer and then to the appropriate control surface servo through an electrical cable, the aircraft becomes 'fly-by-wire'. However, it is likely that the B-2A uses fibre-optic strands rather than cables, as these are more resistant to electro-magnetic pulses (EMP) associated with nuclear explosions; the DFCS is then known as 'fly-by-light'. Such systems are usually weighty as they do not require shielding from EMP.

The control surfaces on the B-2 – simple flaps – are all located on the trailing edge of the wing and controlled via the DFCS. With the aircraft's centre of gravity well back, the flaps can be used to improve lift for take-off and landing. Two further pairs of flaps are located above the engine exhausts and can be used to provide a simple form of thrust-vectoring. This probably has its most effective use at low speeds, to improve pitch control.

The overall shape of the aircraft has been designed to conventional aerodynamic and structural logic but it also has much impact on the inherent stealthiness of the aircraft. The reasons behind the F-117A's multi-faceted, flat-plate surface have already been described. Ideally, a diamond-shaped structure would reflect the least of radar signals. The B-2 has two major flat reflecting surfaces – the wing and the straight lines of the leading and trailing edges. In an apparent contradiction of the foregoing, the curves, or smooth contours, over the rest of the surface constantly change radius in order to maximize electro-magnetic scatter. The trick – and it is a very complicated trade-off, only possible by the use of supercomputers – is the way in which the laws of aerodynamics and electro-magnetics have been compromised to produce an aircraft which flies yet presents the lowest possible radar cross-section.

The powerplant of the B-2, four General Electric F118-GE-100 non-afterburning turbofans, is derived from the lineage of the GE's F110 turbofan used on some F-16s and later marks of the F-14 and the experience of the CFM56 civil turbofan, developed in col-

laboration with SNECMA of France. The size of the engine fan dictates the size of the air intakes and vice versa. Again, the design compromise was made. The available size of the intakes, compatible with its stealthiness, dictated by the use of 'S'-bends in the intake and the use of reflecting surfaces and radar absorbent material (RAM), indicated an engine size more usually associated with a fighter than a bomber or civil transport. Another feature of the intakes is the slit-inlet below the main inlet on the wing surface to skim away the boundary-layer airflow, drastically reducing the chance of turbulent air causing engine flame-outs.

Where engines are concerned, what goes in must come out, and there, in the exhausts, another compromise had to be made. It is not the heat of the exhaust *per se* which is the problem, but the radiation from the hot air and water vapour emitted by the engines. These are the two main products which modern infra-red (IR) missile seekers and aircraft infra-red search-and-track (IRST) sensors (as fitted to current Soviet interceptors) are looking for. Thus the key to reducing the chance of detection by such systems is to dissipate these effects as soon as possible after they depart from the aircraft. To this end, the engines exhaust over the wing into a trough, the sides of which have been carefully contoured as mentioned above. It is likely that flow-mixers have been fitted to the engines to permit the cold bypass air, as well as air from the boundary-layer slit at the intakes, to mix with the hot exhaust gases. This is helped by making the exhaust nozzles of a flatter cross-section, allowing the cold air to mix more quickly. As the airflow exits the trough, it is probable that the vortices created will promote the mixing of the air still further.

The material from which the B-2 is constructed is also part of the stealth compromise. The exact composition of the structure is of course highly classified, but it is likely that artificial fibre such as graphite (carbon) and Kevlar are used for as many of the load-bearing structures as possible. Composites are also widely used in the skinning of the aircraft, generally with a Nomex honeycomb structure beneath, thus removing the need for stringers or stiffeners. All these materials are by nature almost radar absorbent, and are known by the acronym RAS (radar absorbent structure).

The very shape of the B-2, from some angles, makes for a reduced visual signature. The colour of the external paintwork, a dark grey, also assists in reducing the aircraft's visibility at a distance. Should that paint be of the 'iron-ball' type mentioned in relation to the F-117, then a further degree of radar absorption is added to the whole. The iron compounds used in the paint, called ferrites, are also used in RAM, as are some organic polymers containing certain salts. The exact details are, again, highly classified, but they cut radar echoes by reflecting the emitted signals back internally and by deflecting them sharply so they do not bounce back to a receiver, or they reflect them back with a change of phase which tends to cancel them out. Different types of RAM use any or all of these techniques and materials and are usually optimized for certain radar frequencies or bands of frequencies. However, in order to be effective, it is vital that they be applied in precise thicknesses and that their consistencies are perfectly matched to particular requirements.

With regard to avionics and armament, the B-2A, unlike the F-117A, does have a radar system – the Hughes APQ-118 low-probability-of-intercept, covert strike radar, conformally mounted in the lower side of the leading edge towards the centre-section of the wing. Navigation equipment includes the Rockwell Collins TCN-250 tacan (tactical air navigation) and the VIR-130A ILS (instrument landing system). Most of the avionics racks are located aft of the crew compartment in the centrebody of the aircraft, for easier access during maintenance. The armament consists of sixteen AGM-131 SRAM IIs or AGM-129 ACMs mounted in eight-round Boeing Advanced Applications Rotary Launchers in each of the two weapons bays, mounted side-by-side in the lower centrebody. Alternative loads include the B61 and B83 free-fall nuclear bombs, the Mk. 36 1,000lb sea mine, the M117 750lb fire bomb or a maximum of 80 Mk. 82 500lb HE bombs.

The B-2A is still in the early stages of its flight test programme and there is still a political battle to be fought for its future. Short of a Russian stealth bomber beyond the Tu-160 'Blackjack', the Northrop B-2 is likely to be the last manned heavy bomber for the next 30 years.

Advanced Tactical Fighter

To best examine the application of stealth, the recent competition to determine the next generation of Advanced Tactical Fighter (ATF) to succeed the USAF's

► This head-on view of the Lockheed/Boeing/General Dynamics YF-22A, the winning type in the USAF's Advanced Tactical Fighter evaluation, shows the angular influence of the F-117A. (Lockheed)

F-15 Eagle may be reviewed. Two airframe contractor teams, led by Lockheed (with Boeing Aerospace and General Dynamics) and Northrop (with McDonnell Douglas), worked on the demonstration and validation (dem/val) phase of the project from October 1986. Two each of the YF-22A and YF-23A prototype air vehicles (PAVs) were built, the first of each type making their maiden flights on 29 September 1990 and 27 August 1990 respectively. In a similar way, the engines for the ATF were also being competitively evaluated, but under separate contracts, awarded in 1983. General Electric developed the YF120 and Pratt & Whitney the YF119 turbofan. Each competing design had one PAV powered by the YF119 and one by the YF120, offering a total of four airframe/engine combinations.

The PAVs were, it was frequently stressed, not for purely competitive evaluation but to demonstrate feasibility and generate information for the definitive requirements. In September 1987 the ATF programme manager, Colonel (now Brigadier General) James A. Fain Jr, told the author that 'the way I will "spec" it is not by airplane but by requirement', specifying that 'it will go so fast, so far, for so long, carry so much fuel and carry so many weapons'. He was emphatic that he would 'not specify "A" or "B" . . .'. The prototypes, he stressed, were 'not a plot'. Thus the good points of each competing design and its systems could, in theory, be melded into one definitive ATF. This might mean a variant of the Lockheed YF-22A or the Northrop YF-23A or it can mean an amalgam of both. According to General Ronald W. Yates, commander of the USAF's Systems Command, during the demonstration/validation (dem/val) phase the YF-23A was 'not going to participate in a fly-off with the YF-22A'. Yet, despite all protestations that the dem/val phase of the ATF was 'part of a risk reduction programme', the reality suggested that the basis for a new tactical fighter must be one or the other. If one considered the options, there could be neither the time nor money to merge the designs. While it is accepted that both the F-14 Tomcat and F-15 Eagle represent the current standard in fighter technology, both airframes are some 20 years old. However much the powerplants, internal weapons systems and avionics have been updated, they are still 'last year's models'. New technologies have posed new threats and these have evolved over that period. These aircraft must be replaced over the next 10–15 years.

However, events moved a long way in the interim. The thaw in the Cold War put a different emphasis on the United States' outlook on the world, which the Gulf War has confirmed, and also on its defence budget. Virtually every major military project is being put under the microscope and, so far, the ATF has survived – albeit with a slight delay in the selection of the contractor teams, which was finally made on 23 April 1991. The award for the full-scale development (FSD) contract was signed in August 1991. On this schedule, initial deliveries should begin about 1996. The original requirement for 750 ATFs was, as expected, reduced – to 640 aircraft.

So what was the USAF looking for in its new fighter? According to Major General Joseph W. Ralston, Director of USAF Tactical Programmes, five major characteristics were required to be demonstrated in one aircraft: low observables (i.e. stealth), enabling the enemy to be sighted first; high manœuvrability and agility; supersonic cruise with military thrust – the so-called 'supercruise'; an adequate payload, comparable to that of the F-15; and sufficient range for all theatres of operation worldwide. The accompanying data table offers a comparison of the two designs and the F-15 benchmark, as far as is possible on estimated figures:

	YF-22A (approx.)	YF-23A (approx.)	F-15C (actual)
Wingspan (ft/m)	42.81/13.05	43.0/13.11	43.6/13.26
Length (ft/m)	63.75/19.43	64.2/19.56	67.4/20.54
Height (ft/m)	18.45/5.62	17.7/5.39	13.9/4.24
Wing area (ft^2/m^2)	608/56.48	830/77.11	950/88.26
Combat T/O weight (lb/kg)	59,500/26,989	62,000/28,123	64,000/19,030
Empty weight (lb/kg)	32,050/14,538	34,000/15,422	37,000/16,783
Internal fuel (lb/kg)	13,455/6,134	25,000/11,340	24,000/10,886

The Lockheed contender, the YF-22A, looked the more conventional of the two, having a 'normal' empennage layout of twin fins and tailplanes. According to Ben Rich, former President of the famous 'Skunk Works' where the two Lockheed PAVs were put together, 'we have stressed agility – we can go to any angle of attack ... we will not depart'.

Yet the YF-22A design is still stealthy. The wing-plan of the YF-22A is of an 'eight-lobe' radar cross-section with most features of the angular design (based on F-117A experience) aligned with the wing leading edges. The tailfins are canted outboard at some 27 degrees. The engines are set in the upper rear fuselage, with the tailplanes masking the exhaust. The air intakes are set beneath the wing's leading edge root extension (LERX) and offer a slight inwardly angled duct to obscure the fan blades from radar reflections.

Northrop's YF-23A offered a different approach, being optimized for speed rather than agility. The wings are of clipped-rhombus form, with the leading edge of the port wing parallel with the trailing edge of the starboard wing and vice versa. The tail surfaces are similarly parallel, in plan view, with the wings, although these are in a different plane. The YF-23A's 'butterfly' tail, referred to by Northrop as 'ruddervators', is canted outward at 45 degrees while the shaping of the wing/fuselage shows more blending than the YF-22A, based on the experience of the B-2A bomber. Certainly, the planform trailing edge of the tail surfaces and rear fuselage exhibit the 'twin-W' serrations of the B-2A.

The engines are mounted about two-thirds the way from the nose, exhausting over the top of the fuselage, shielding the hot engine parts from below. This, however, will have added extra weight because of the need for heat-resistant materials along the trough and also the need for strength against sonic fatigue. Without a defined LERX, Northrop opted for a hexagonal nose profile and the air intakes are located immediately below the wing/fuselage junction. This allows for a more defined 'S'-duct to take intake air to the engines and more effective shielding of the fan.

For its air superiority role, the ATF is required to match the weapons load of the F-15 Eagle – four AIM-9 Sidewinder and four AIM-120 AMRAAM – but must carry it internally. This concept goes back to the mid-1950s and the Convair F-106 Delta Dart. In order to accommodate the required missile armament, the Lockheed team has opted for weapons bays for the Sidewinders on the intake ducts, with AIM-120 carriage in a ventral bay. The Northrop solution had two ventral weapons bays in tandem, with the Sidewinders ahead of the AMRAAMs. Both designs have provision for an internal gun, still a necessity in air combat. This weapon has already been specified by the USAF – the 20mm M61A2 Vulcan cannon. While tried and tested, it is now some 30 years old and one cannot help but wonder whether or not the Cased Telescoped Gun will be retrofitted in the future.

The avionics were an integral part of the ATF and neither contender ignored this in its bid. The USAF stressed the importance of using leading-edge technology, such as VHSIC (Very High Speed Integrated Circuits), Ada software and advanced data processors with highly integrated common modules linked by databus. In addition, work done on the INEWS (Integrated Electronic Warfare System) and ICNIA (Integrated Communications/Navigation/Identification Avionics) programmes was being incorporated, together with work on shared antennae for several systems and cockpit displays which show integrated data from several sources with sensor fusion.

As prime contractor on the YF-22A team, Lockheed has overall responsibility for avionics system design and architecture. Ben Rich told the author that 'the avionics, surprisingly, has given us the least problems'.

► This profile view of the YF-22A highlights the large fins and the deep forward fuselage, its large one-piece canopy offering superb all-round visibility. (Lockheed)

► Looking down on the YF-22A, the parallel leading and trailing edges of the wings and tailplanes, as well as of the leading edge of the air intakes, become apparent. The size of the fins is also emphasized here. (Lockheed)

Within the team, Lockheed are dealing with the avionics mission software, aperture development, cockpit, core architecture components and system integration. The responsibility for avionics testing rests with the Boeing third of the partnership; the company has a ground laboratory and a Boeing 757 flying test-bed. Additionally, Boeing is responsible for the radar (with Westinghouse and Texas Instruments on the system itself), the infra-red search/track (IRST) with General Electric and the mission processing software (with Hughes). The General Dynamics portion of the avionics covers communications, navigation and identification (with TRW) and electronic warfare development (with the Lockheed Sanders/General Electric joint venture team). Additionally, GD is providing the stores management and vehicle management sub-systems.

For the YF-23A, the Northrop/McDonnell Douglas team decided to use an avionics ground prototype (AGP) to demonstrate the various concepts offered for an FSD aircraft. Both radar hardware and radar software have been integrated and demonstrated on this AGP. The data used have included information recorded during flight trials on board a BAC-111 airliner specially modified as a flying avionics laboratory. The integrated navigation, communications and identification system has also been exercised with integrated signal and radar processing. By April 1990, demonstrations had proved that over 500,000 lines of Ada software codes could be run on the AGP and, also, that a number of common modules could be interchanged to perform a wide range of tasks. Such modules can reduce the number of 'black boxes' within an aircraft, creating a more flexible avionics system. Additionally, sensor data fusion has been demonstrated, with data recorded from sensors on board the BAC-111, as well as the integration of an advanced 32-bit general-purpose processor.

Just as the airframe manufacturers were anxious to convince the USAF that their aircraft met ATF requirements, so, too, were the engine manufacturers. Development of the competing YF119 and YF120 powerplants began in 1983, and the dem/val went well for both General Electric and Pratt & Whitney. A particular aspect of these engines is their ability to perform well above the speed of sound without having to use afterburner; the F-14 and F-15 can barely exceed Mach 1 without recourse to reheat. Just prior to the decision, General Electric reported that the YF-22A PAV equipped with the YF120 engine reached Mach 1.58 on supercruise. The supercruise speed on the YF-23A PAV remains classified; so, as the GE spokesman told the author, 'you know it exceeded Mach 1.58'. The YF119-powered YF-23A reached Mach 1.43.

The YF120 engine is said to have met all USAF requirements, not only in supercruise, but in thrust-vectoring, maximum afterburner take-off, aerial refuelling, transients and airstarts. Specific details on flights are not available from GE. The Pratt & Whitney YF119 logged in excess of 150 flight hours in 65 flights with both PAVs. A company spokesman said that, during dem/val, 'the YF119 was always ready to fly [and] had no in-flight shut-downs and no aborts'. He maintained

▲ The thrust-vectoring nozzle arrangement of the engines of the YF-22A can be clearly seen in this view of the aircraft over the Mojave Desert. (Lockheed)

◄ The underside of the YF-22A here just reveals the two long weapons bays for the carriage of AIM-120 AMRAAM missiles; the Sidewinder bays are on either side of the forward engine intake trunk. Note the cutaway rear fuselage for the thrust-vectoring nozzles. (Lockheed)

that the engine demonstrated total reliability and 'had no throttle restrictions anywhere in the envelope'. In short, he reported, it 'met 100 per cent of ATF requirements'. While P&W have admitted that their engine is smaller than their rival's, they note that a production version with a larger fan is in parallel development. This 'will offer more thrust than the ATF will ever need'.

The US Navy had been taking an interest in both PAVs throughout dem/val, and Navy members were included in the ATF Source Selection Board. The idea had been that the Navy adopt a carrier-based version of the ATF to replace the F-14 Tomcat. By way of reciprocation, the USAF were (until just prior to its cancellation in January 1991) considering a land-based version of the A-12 Advanced Tactical Aircraft to replace the F-111. The decision that the A-12 would not meet USAF requirements and the uncertainties over funding for the naval ATF led the USN to convert its firm requirement to an option. This was reflected in the competing 'best and final offers' in the bidding procedure.

For both airframe and engine manufacturers, this was a 'winner takes all' competition. The two competing teams put their proposals to the USAF on 1 January 1991, and their best and final offers in mid-March, when the decision-makers began considering their verdict. As many of the factors contributing to the 'blackness' of the ATF programme have now been removed, the author believes that the concept of not opting for either the F-22 or F-23 would now be less

▲ This composite view shows the launch sequence of an AIM-9M Sidewinder from the YF119-powered first YF-22A prototype in November 1990, over the US Naval Weapons Center at China Lake. (Lockheed)

► Air-to-air refuelling capabilities were demonstrated by the YF-22A with both the KC-135 (illustrated) and the KC-10 tanker aircraft during the evaluation process. (Lockheed)

◄ The 'blended' approach adopted by the Northrop/McDonnell Douglas team for their YF-23A contender for the ATF programme is apparent in this view of the aircraft over the Mojave Desert. (MACAIR)

► This head-on view of the YF-23A shows the 'ruddervator' concept of the empennage, as well as the smooth blending of contours. (Northrop)

constrictive – at least as far as the airframe was concerned. Ben Rich also believed that the USAF had to opt for one or other of the airframes. He told the author in 1990 that Lockheed works to the concept that 'when you build a prototype, it should be very close to a production airplane. If you lay our [F-22] production airplane next to our prototype, the loft lines are almost identical.' He accepted that internal changes would have to be made as well as to the composition of the airframe. He said, 'We'll have more composites to save weight and we'll have to improve the avionics.'

This is the one area where a possible melding of

◄ This view shows both YF-23A prototypes in the air together, highlighting the profile and plan views of the aircraft. The design is less conventional than that of the YF-22A and is probably centred more on the air-to-air environment than on the aircraft's multi-role capability. (Northrop)

► One of the YF119-PW-100 development engines fitted with a generic two-dimensional thrust-vectoring nozzle, seen running with full afterburner at Pratt & Whitney's test facilities at West Palm Beach. (P&W)

competing solutions to the ATF requirement could occur – the avionics and sensors field. With the vast number of subcontractors participating in the programme, selection will, undoubtedly, be made on the basis of how well they do in the dem/val phase. The main ATF avionics are, after all, not on board the prototypes but on airliner test-beds.

Despite the euphoria over the successful air campaign over the Gulf, the reality is that the US defence budget must be reduced. Yet older aircraft have to be replaced. Cost is always the enemy and, to borrow an old DoD cliché, they want 'more bang per buck' – but with more capability. Research and development costs money, and production aircraft cost more money. At the end of the day, we could see a situation where the FSD phase is completed but production is shelved. That is one scenario, and it could also be influenced by the appearance of a Soviet fighter beyond the MiG-29 or Sukhoi Su-27. These aircraft are the other benchmarks against which the ATF was, in reality, evaluated. Another factor which probably played an important part in the selection procedure was the status of the contractors. Lockheed was running out of military programmes fast. Northrop was being caned by the DoD on B-2 costs, while McDonnell Douglas had the dual problem of on-going military work and being part of the failed USN A-12 team.

The decision was announced by the USAF on 23 April 1991 in favour of the Lockheed team and the F-22, powered by Pratt & Whitney's F119 engine. Now (the author notes lightly) all that has to be done is turn a dem/val prototype into a production aircraft. A side issue, but none the less emotive, will be the choice of name for the F-22. With a previous Lockheed product named Lightning (the P-38 of the Second World War) and the UK's English Electric Lightning now out of RAF service, the odds are on 'Lightning II', after the fashion of the F-4 Phantom II, the A-7 Corsair II and A-10 Thunderbolt II.

Advanced Tactical Aircraft

So far we have looked at stealth aircraft which have flown and, indeed, in one case, been successful in combat. It has been emphasized that in each instance the mix of stealth and operational capability is a complex technical compromise. Yet, inasmuch as they are out there, flying, they are successes, and two if not three of these aircraft will be operational into the next century. One stealth project which dissolved in a sea of recrimination was the US Navy's Advanced Tactical Aircraft (ATA) project, the General Dynamics/McDonnell Douglas A-12 Avenger II.

Without entering into the legal arguments surrounding the project (which continue at the time of writing) it is worth recording the details of the aircraft itself, such as are available. The A-12 was designed to replace the ageing A-6 Intruder, the USN's premier carrier-borne attack bomber. For a while the USAF was con-

◄ This composite photograph shows the launch of an AIM-120 AMRAAM from the YF120-powered second prototype YF-22A on 20 December 1990, over the Pacific Missile Test Center near Point Mugu. (Lockheed)

► In the cancelled McDonnell Douglas/General Dynamics A-12 Avenger II Advanced Attack Aircraft for the US Navy (shown here in model form), the aerodynamics of stealth were taken to their logical conclusion in the form of the delta flying wing. The only major protuberance is the canopy. (MACAIR)

sidering a variant as a replacement for its F-111 strike fighters, as a quid pro quo for the Navy's consideration of the ATF as an F-14 Tomcat replacement. In the event, the USAF decided that the A-12 would not meet its requirements shortly before the Navy's cancellation was announced. Litigation apart, the cancellation of the A-12 has led to a revised Navy requirement study for an A-6 replacement, under the designation AX, which implies that the need for stealth is not as important as was previously the case.

The US Navy announced the selection of the General Dynamics/McDonnell Douglas team to develop the A-12 in December 1987. It was a Christmas present that would turn sour. The companies were awarded a fixed-price incentive contract, valued at $4.379 billion, for the work. In November 1988 the USAF awarded the companies a $7.9 million contract for a concept definition study of the A-12 as a possible F-111 replacement. The primary missions which the A-12 was to be called upon to perform were varied – strike, anti-surface warfare, interdiction/search-and-destroy and the air-delivery of sea mines. Among the secondary missions envisaged for the aircraft included anti-air warfare (as a long-range bomber destroyer rather than an air combat fighter), reconnaissance and electronic intelligence (elint) gathering. There would be a significant avionics growth potential to allow for these and other alternative roles.

If the designs of the F-117A and B-2B were revolutionary in appearance (the F-22A is actually reasonably conventional), the concept of the A-12 was positively science fiction – a flying delta wing with no vertical control surfaces at all. Cheek air scoops in the lower part of the leading edge flanked a conformal radar, while the only protuberance above the wing upper surface was a well-faired two-man cockpit. The two GE F412 turbofans, derived from the GE F404, were located in the wing centre-section, exhausting under the trailing edge. All weapons were planned for internal carriage, although some sources have mentioned the possible use of external stores when necessary. The A-12 would have been capable of carrying all the weapons currently used by the A-6E, plus air-to-air missiles. An extremely accurate nav/attack system would allow weapons delivery with 'exceptional precision'.

The A-12 was a large aircraft, with a wingspan of about 70ft, a length of 37ft, a maximum depth of 7ft and a wing area of some 1,300 sq. ft. The radar cross-section was said to be one-twelfth that of the A-6 and one-fifth that of the F/A-18 Hornet. The span was limited by the need to be able to position two aircraft on adjacent catapults, a peculiarly naval requirement

◀ This head-on view of the A-12 model reveals the underwing air intakes, suggesting underwing exhausts, the deepness of the structure (to enable the weapons to be carried internally) and two conformal radar antennae in the midwing leading edge. (MACAIR)

to add to the criteria to be traded off in the design stage. Similarly, the undercarrige was to be of a strength required to sustain deck landings, and an arrester hook was to be fitted. Doubtless a rectractable air-to-air refuelling point was positioned close to the nose on the upper surface. Survivability in combat was high on the list of criteria to be incorporated into the design. Apart from a variety of passive sensors and the stealth technology, radar and missile warning systems and electronic countermeasures (ECM) were included. Additionally, many other passive features such as inert nitrogen-charged fuel cells, dry-bay fire-suppression systems and multiple, redundant hydraulic and electrical systems were to be included.

As the A-12 never actually flew, measuring its performance is difficult. However, it was designed to achieve a significantly greater combat range than that of the A-6E, in the region of 80 per cent. With the weapons being carried internally (a maximum payload some 40 per cent greater than that of the A-6E was envisaged), variation in weapons loads was expected to have little effect on the combat radius. Maximum instantaneous turn rate was to have exceeded that of both the A-6E and F/A-18, while sustained turn capability was better than the A-6's and better than the F/A-18's without afterburning.

Apart from the problems of costings and timescale, excessive weight seems to have been the downfall of the A-12. Initially the weight seems to have been underestimated and, although a weight-reduction programme was initiated, it is understood that the weapons payloads could not reach the requirements of the Navy; to have met these would have sent an already spiralling cost up further. The USAF divorced itself from the programme in December 1990, saying that the aircraft would have engine trouble in hot-and-high situations. Some observers indicated, unofficially, that the simple fact that it was 'a Navy airplane' was its undoing. Left with the Navy alone, in an era of declining budgets, the rising costs and delays were considered unacceptable. So, on 7 January 1991, US Defense Secretary Richard Cheney 'pulled the plug' on the A-12 and cancelled the project.

In the interim, until the A-6/A-12 replacement, the AX, is decided, the US Navy is faced with re-winging further A-6Es and ordering more F/A-18s, some C/D models initially but with the prospect of new E/F models. As to the AX, little is known of the Navy's thoughts at the time of writing, beyond the suggestion that stealth will not be the all-governing criterion it was on the A-12. It is known, however, that Lockheed are keen to promote a variant of the F-22A, while Grumman appear to be fighting a losing battle to convince the Navy that the F-14 Tomcat has growth potential and cost benefits. It will be the mid-1990s before any decision is taken.

Light Helicopter

After many years of technology development and a competitive dem/val phase, the US Army finally decided on its replacement Light Helicopter (LH, formerly LHX) on 5 April 1991. The contractors selected were known as 'The First Team', led by Boeing Helicopters and Sikorsky Aircraft and formed in 1985. The LH, now officially designated RAH-66A Comanche, will be used to replace almost 3,000 AH-1 Cobra, OH-6 Cayuse and OH-58 Kiowa light attack and reconnaissance helicopters, although not on a one-for-one basis as only 1,292 are currently planned. It has a multi-role capability and is planned to complement the AH-64 Apache. It is the first stealth helicopter, its projected low-observable characteristics including a reduced radar cross-section, integrated infra-red suppression and low acoustic/visual signatures.

The RAH-66A Comanche is an all-composite helicopter with a five-bladed, bearingless main rotor system

▶
The US Army's approach to the stealth helicopter is revealed in this mock-up of the winning design for the Light Helicopter competition – the Boeing/Sikorsky RAH-66A Comanche. (Sikorsky)

and a 'fantail' anti-torque rotor system, similar to the fenestron used in the Aérospatiale Gazelle and Dauphin helicopters. The twin-engine powerplant is US Government furnished equipment – the LHTEC (a teaming of Allison and Garrett) T800-LHT-800 turboshaft, rated at 925shp. For the reconnaissance mission the helicopter will carry an armament of one GE 20mm Gatling-type gun with 500 rounds (with a maximum rate of fire of 1,500rds/min) and four AGM-114 Hellfire anti-armour missiles, plus two AIM-92 Stinger AAMs, for self-defence, in an internal weapons bay. For attack missions, an external pylon can be fitted to offer a maximum armament of up to fourteen Hellfires or eighteen Stingers or sixty-two 2.75in FFAR (folding-fin aerial rockets), plus the 20mm gun.

The two-man helicopter is equipped with a sophisticated avionics suite comprising a targeting system and a night/adverse weather flying system. The former consists of a second-generation, focal-plane-array FLIR, a low-light television, a laser rangefinder/designator and an aided target detection/classification system. The latter involves the FLIR, image intensifiers and a wide-field-of-view, helmet-mounted sight.

The Comanche will be developed in two phases: dem/val and FSD, lasting some eight years in total. Four prototypes are planned for the dem/val phase with a further two later. The Comanche is scheduled to make its maiden flight in September 1994, and an initial operating capability for the first US Army unit equipped with the type is planned for December 1998.

Stealth Spy

With the demise of the Lockheed SR-71 'Blackbird' Mach 3 strategic reconnaissance aircraft, many people wondered if satellites could really replace this capability. While the USAF 'kept mum' over the existence of any stealth replacement, it was reported in the prestigious US magazine *Aviation Week & Space Technology*

▶
This preliminary cutaway of the RAH-66A Comanche shows the retractable undercarriage, the internal weapons bay (with two Hellfire anti-tank missiles and one Stinger air-to-air missile) and the engine/dynamic train configuration. For some missions, stub pylons can be fitted to increase the weapons load. (Sikorsky)

▶
A BAe study is looking at ways of improving the Tornado IDS beyond the GR.4 upgrade. This is one of several configurations being investigated to improve 'stealthiness' and increase combat radius to 650nm. (BAe Military Aircraft)

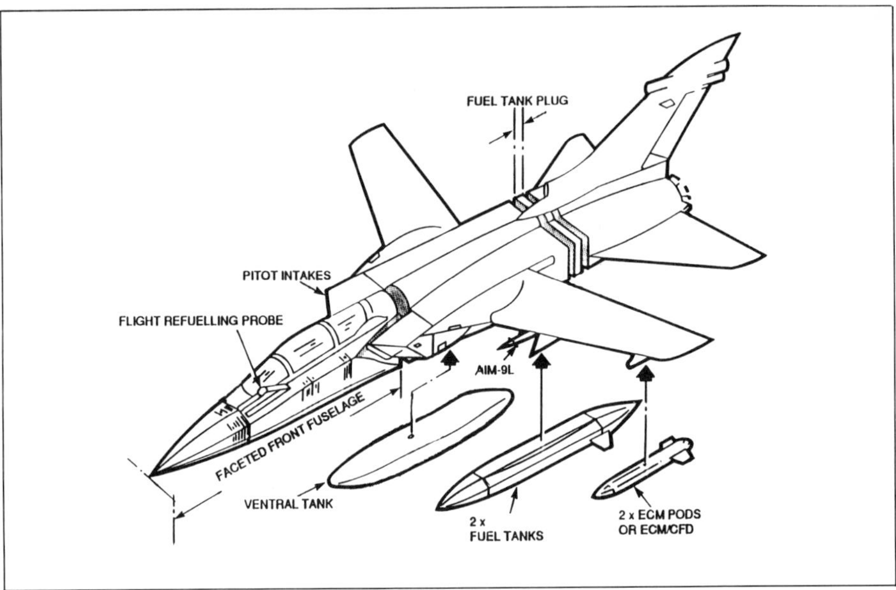

in June 1991 that a stealth reconnaissance aircraft, designated TR-3A 'Black Manta', existed and, indeed, may have supported the F-117As in their operations during the Gulf War. At the time of writing, there has been no official confirmation of this aircraft's existence, but, as its nickname suggests, it is of a triangular format, similar to the A-12, but with inwardly canted fins (called 'rudderatrons') to provide control in both roll and yaw planes. According to *Aviation Week*, the TR-3A is based on a Northrop design known as the Tactical High-Altitude Penetrator (THAP), developed under a USAF stealth technology programme of the 1970s called Covert Survivable In-weather Reconnaissance/Strike (CSIRS). Some 25–30 TR-3As are said to have been built by Northrop and the aircraft have the ability to provide real-time reconnaissance imagery. The TR-3A derivative of the THAP (which is understood to have been first flown in 1981) was reportedly contracted for in 1982.

Said to be the size of an F/A-18 Hornet, the TR-3A is thought to be some 42ft long with a wingspan of some 60–65ft. The triangular shape of the aircraft employs rounded, blended surfaces and RAM. It is thought to be powered by a pair of GE F404 non-afterburning turbofan engines, but with a quieter noise-print than those of the F-117A. The intakes are positioned above the wings, as in the B-2, while the exhausts are forward of the wing trailing edge, shielding them from ground-based acoustic and IR detection. The aircraft's range is reported to be in excess of 3,000nm.

If these reports are true, then it is possible that a B model may already be under development with applications for both the strategic and tactical reconnaissance roles.

The Future

Most of the types described in this chapter have been designed with the accent on low observability. The technology has been proved both in peacetime and under combat conditions. However, if all the indications are correct, it will be possible to design more conventional looking aircraft and yet maintain Ben Rich's six disciplines of stealth. Sweden's new JAS.39 Gripen fighter, although never advertised as a stealth aircraft, is small enough to go a long way towards meeting some of the requirements, as are, one could argue, the French Rafale and the European Fighter Aircraft. The use of RAM and RAS, as well as of improved electronic warfare wizardry, will provide other aspects. It proves the point. The YF-22 is more like the F-15 than its rival, the YF-23. The AX replacement for the A-12 is expected to be less revolutionary in appearance. This is now possible. As far as the US forces are concerned, stealth is going to be with us well into the next century.

KEY TECHNOLOGIES

While the impression given in the previous chapter may be that stealth aircraft are 'the only game in town', this is far from the truth. Cost alone limits the ability of many customers to buy and that of manufacturers to develop such aircraft. Thus conventional wisdom continues to be refined and, wherever possible, stealth characteristics are built into designs that are, to the untutored eye, evolutionary rather than revolutionary. Apart from the development and application of technologies in the low-observability arena, there are many other areas where advances will affect aircraft design and improve performance. Some of these, such as fly-by-wire (FBW), have already been touched upon in the previous chapter.

Flight Control Systems

The whole aspect of aircraft flight control has been influenced by the development of FBW and the rapid miniaturization of the associated processors (computers). Taken as a whole, which includes the design of the aircraft itself to take advantage of FBW, this subject is known as Active Control Technology. The first combat aircraft to take advantage of such developments was the General Dynamics F-16 Fighting Falcon. In order to improve the fighter's agility – vital for air combat – the traditional values of a stable and balanced aircraft have been discarded. The basic aircraft is now intentionally designed to be unstable and it is able to fly only because the on-board flight control processors monitor the aircraft's status (i.e. its attitude, speed and direction in flight) some 40 times per second (on average) and continually adjust the control surfaces to prevent the aircraft from deviating uncontrollably from the pilot's intended flight path. This concept is known as 'relaxed stability'.

Designers have now found that moving the wing aft and bringing the tailplanes forward of the wings, to become canard foreplanes (more usually referred to as canards), will enhance manœuvrability as well as improve lift. Additionally, this configuration allows the aircraft's attitude to be partially decoupled from its flight path. Thus, while flying straight-and-level, the aircraft can 'point' upward or downward or to one side or the other. It is also possible, within limits, to move sideways or vertically without turning or tilting, and to turn without banking the aircraft. Such abilities enhance air combat in that they improve the weapons-aiming ability of the pilot/aircraft combination.

▶ In order to mature a number of key technologies for the aircraft of the 1990s and beyond, British Aerospace embarked on the Experimental Aircraft Programme and built a prototype aircraft known as EAP. It encompasses new materials, active control technology, a 'glass cockpit' and many other features. It subsequently became a technology demonstrator for the European Fighter Aircraft. (BAe Military Aircraft)

◄ In a joint US-German programme, attracting Nunn Amendment funding from the United States, Rockwell and MBB/DASA are conducting an Enhanced Fighter Maneuverability (EFM) programme at high angles of attack with the X-31 research aircraft. Note the engine thrust 'paddles' aft of the exhaust for thrust-vectoring in flight. (MBB/DASA)

The AJ.37 Viggen was the first combat aircraft to be designed with canards, and its successor, the JAS.39 Gripen, currently under development, is similarly configured. Both the European Fighter Aircraft (EFA) and the French Rafale have also been designed with canards. Indeed, the technology can even be retrofitted. Dassault (and other manufacturers) offer the installation of fixed canards as part of an upgrade package for the Mirage III/V/50 series of fighters. As yet, neither the Soviet Union nor the United States have adopted the configuration for an operational design. The US has, however, incorporated it on the Grumman X-29 forward-swept wing development aircraft and the Rockwell International/MBB (now Deutsche Aerospace) X-31 experimental aircraft used in the Enhanced Fighter Maneuverability (EFM) programme.

As mentioned earlier, FBW technology is, even now, being superseded by the use of fibre-optic cables to transmit the signals between the pilot's controls and the flight control system. Instead of using an electrical signal down a wire, a light signal is used through the fibre-optic cable. This is known as fly-by-light, or FBL.

◄ The Mission Adaptive Wing (MAW) has no hinged flaps, spoilers or other control surfaces to break the smooth contour of its upper surface. Advanced design variable-camber mechanisms, coupled to digital flight computers and sensors, regulate the contour of the fibreglass material covering the wing. Thus the aerodynamic shape of the wing can be changed in flight to accommodate the needs of the mission from subsonic through to supersonic speeds. The MAW is now flying on a NASA F-111. (Boeing Military Aircraft)

▶
This view of the cockpit of an F-16C shows the move away from traditional analogue instrumentation to the use of the multi-function display (MFD). Note the wide-angle HUD and the side-stick controller. (General Dynamics)

The advantages of FBL are that fibre-optic cables are lighter, have a greater data capacity, make no detectable emissions and are immune to the effects of the EMP generated by nuclear explosions.

The advent of this technology allows the designers to look again at the way control surfaces are used on aircraft. Already on many aircraft the tailplanes, which had elevator control surfaces, and fins, which had rudder surfaces, have been changed. Now the whole surface moves, rather than a specific part of it, in response to the control input. Similarly, on the wings, the aileron function can now be assumed by split flaps in the same position, moving up or down in response to control input.

NASA in the United States has been looking at the Mission Adaptive Wing. In essence, this is a wing that adjusts its aerofoil section in response to the pilot's control inputs. This effectively removes the need for leading- and trailing-edge flaps and ailerons, saving weight and simplifying construction. Their associated mechanical and hydraulic systems are embedded within the wing. Tests on a modified F-111 have yielded improvements in range, altitude and agility. It has also been found that structural stress can be reduced by varying the wing profile, so that more lift is generated close to the wing root when necessary.

Into the Cockpit

The developments in flight control bring us neatly to the hub of the aircraft – the cockpit and the 'Driver, Airframe' – alias the pilot. Over the past fifteen years we have seen a move away from the traditional method of displaying vital flight information to the pilot. During the 1960s, one could look into any aircraft cockpit, be it a fighter, airliner or helicopter, and recognize the 'basic six' configuration of instruments – altimeter, air speed indicator (ASI), artificial horizon, direction indicator (i.e. compass display), rate-of-climb-and-descent indicator and turn-and-slip indicator. This combination had been established some 40 years earlier and is still used in many civil types. Today, these 'old-fashioned' instruments have all but disappeared from military aircraft. As technology has improved, the information displayed on four of these different 'clock-faces' is now presented on one instrument, the flight situation indicator now combining the functions of the artificial horizon, the altimeter, the ASI and the compass. For combat aircraft, the need for the pilot to keep looking out of the cockpit led to the development of the head-up display (HUD) to present this and other information (usually relating to navigation and weapons aiming) on a transparent screen in front of him at eye-level. In the way technicians love to tag everything with 'buzz phrases' or acronyms, the common-or-garden instrument panel is now called a head-down display, or HDD.

The wealth of information displayed on the HDD and the number of control buttons and switches required are vast, whether it be on a fighter aircraft, a tactical transport aircraft or a SAR helicopter. In addition to the flight information mentioned above, there is all the engine instrumentation, fuel gauges, oil pressure and temperature indicators and the throttles; the more engines the aircraft has, the more dials the HDD requires. There are also the undercarriage selection switches, the radar and navigation system displays and controls, the various radio controls, the weapons management system and display, the electronic warfare displays (of which more later), the cockpit environmental systems ... the list is endless. As technology has developed new systems, space has to be found in the cockpit to include a status display and/or control. No wonder technical qualifications for pilots have risen dramatically.

But where technology produces an ergonomic problem, it soon comes up with a sensible solution. The rapid miniaturization of computers, combined with expansions in memory capacity and processing speed and the development of cathode ray tube (CRT) displays and followed by the availability of liquid crystal displays (LCDs), has led to the innovative 'glass cockpit'. Placing two, three or four CRT or LCD panels in front of him with a set of push-button controls around the edge gives the pilot the means to call up the information he needs via a formatted menu. No longer are all the dials and displays around the cockpit needed.

Gone, too, is the need for a periodic survey of the various major system displays in the cockpit to ensure that all is well: the computer which drives the main multi-function displays (MFDs) does this. If there is a problem in a specific system, a series of small but highly visible hazard warning lights is located on either side of the HUD control panel. Known universally by pilots as 'attention-getters', each light relates to a particular system. So, for example, when the 'Fire' and 'Hydraulics' lights flash, the pilot can then quickly punch his buttons on the appropriate display to see the exact nature and location of the problem.

For the pilot of the combat aircraft, there is a further refinement. In today's environment, once an aircraft is engaged in a weapons delivery run or a dog-fight, the last thing the pilot wishes to be doing is looking down into his cockpit, for example to change his armament panel from bombs to air-to-air missiles or guns or to change radio frequencies. The odds are that by then the 'bad guy' will have shot him down. As he looks ahead in the cockpit, his flight information is there on his HUD, while his hands are grasping the engine throttles and the control column. By adding two or three extra switches to both these controls, the pilot is now able to activate the most vital systems needed for air combat. This technique is known as Hands-On-Throttle-And-Stick, or HOTAS.

Cockpit development never stops. Already companies have developed first-generation helmet-mounted sights to allow the faster aiming of guns or missiles. Basically, as the pilot looks at his target, he presses a button on his HOTAS controls and the location of the

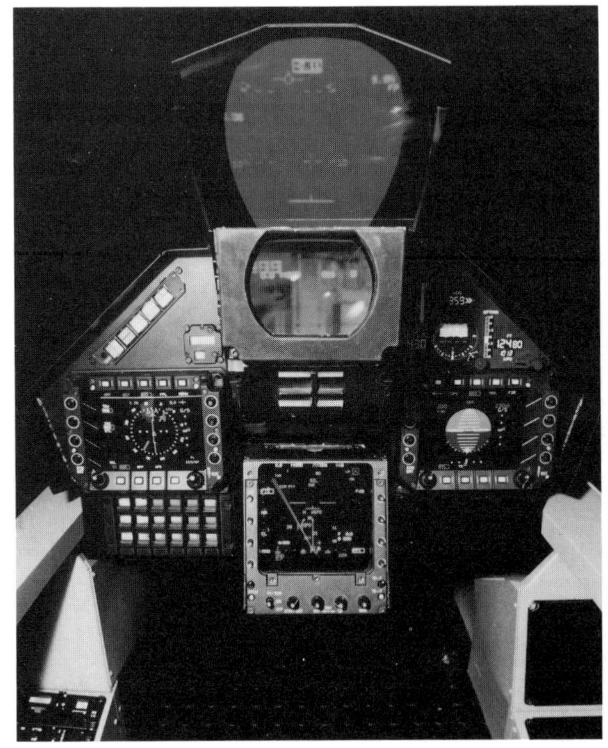

target is passed to the weapons computer and the gun or missile is fired. Now, manufacturers are looking towards producing a mini-HUD attached to the pilot's helmet, which will continue to feed him information while he is moving his head within the cockpit, searching the sky for the 'bad guys'.

The layout of the cockpit itself is changing. In most aircraft the pilot's control column (or joystick) is located between his legs in a central position. Now, with the advent of FBW and removal of the mechanical linkages, it is no longer necessary to locate it there and it has moved to the starboard side console and is referred to as a side-stick controller, notably in the F-16, which began the trend. Again, in the F-16, the pilot's ejection seat has been angled backwards slightly. The reason for this particular innovation is to increase the pilot's G tolerance. As the pilot pulls G in air combat, the blood still tends to rush to the feet, despite his anti-G suit. With the body more 'laid back', the blood finds it harder to move towards the lower extremities. (The author can testify to its effectiveness, having flown in the back seat of an F-16B in 1990. However, he admits to declining the invitation to join the '9G Club' being more than happy with 5.5G.) Both these innovations are included in the cockpits of current fighters under development.

Materials

In order to progress, military aircraft designers have waged a constant campaign to find materials which are both light and strong enough to withstand the advancing stresses of higher speeds and improved agility. From the early years of the Second World War to the late 1960s, aluminium and its associated alloys reigned supreme, with steel derivatives and titanium being used for specialized applications. Throughout the 1970s and 1980s, manufacturer's criteria continued to demand reduced aircraft weight and improved flight performance. In addition, these materials from which combat aircraft are constructed must be able to withstand the rigours of many extreme environmental conditions and, increasingly, lend themselves to rapid repair of battle damage in the field. This latter point is of vital importance for, as the Gulf War of 1991

◄ Some ten years beyond the F-16 is the Mirage 2000-5, and this mock-up of the cockpit shows how the MFD has taken over, along with the HUD. (Sextant Avionique)

► This Lockheed concept takes the cockpit into the twenty-first century with six flat-panel, colour MFDs and a wide-field-of-view HUD, plus the pilot's helmet-mounted display. The programmable nature of the displays eliminates the need for dedicated instrumentation and increases the amount of display space in order to accommodate the increased information received via the aircraft's more sophisticated sensors. (Lockheed)

showed, yet again, wars today are over in a matter of months, if not days; and air forces must fight them with the equipment they have in service: there is no time to wait the two or three years it takes to build a modern military aircraft in order to replace combat attrition.

The use of composite materials has already been mentioned in the previous chapter. Their introduction into the aerospace industry came as a result of their reduced weight, compared with comparable metal parts. Any stealth qualities they bought with them were an additional bonus. Indeed, by using composites, the designers are able significantly to improve the design of aircraft. These materials can be configured into compound shapes and curves which are costly, if not impossible, to produce with metals. The author remembers well, in the late 1960s, seeing parts for the Hawker Siddeley (now BAe) Buccaneer naval strike aircraft being machined out of solid ingots of metal, in order to achieve the complex shape required at the appropriate strength. It was a costly and wasteful process but, at the time, it was the only way of achieving the required results.

The introduction of the computer into both the drawing office and the manufacturing plant has enabled designers to take maximum advantage of the new materials coming on stream. Computer-Aided Design (CAD) offers new flexibility and new opportunities by allowing designers to explore, create and integrate composite structures into new aircraft, and, when the design of an aircraft and its components are 'frozen', Computer-Aided Manufacture (CAM) allows these complex shapes to be produced in large quantities to the high tolerances required.

Composite materials consist of substances such as glass, boron, plastic and carbon (graphite) fibres which are moulded in an epoxy resin (known as a matrix) to produce structural components. The material is light and strong and the resulting components are resistant to buckling under compression and corrosion. As noted above, they can be moulded into complex shapes. They are usually delivered in a form known as 'pre-preg' – as tape or fabric impregnated with the matrix which will bind the fibres together. Depending on the component to be produced, the composite material is either hand-laid on to moulds (for large surface areas such as wing skins, panels or fuselage sides) or fed into a computer-controlled winding machine (as is used to produce composite rotor blades for helicopters), before being 'cured' in a special oven (called an autoclave) under specific conditions of temperature and pressure. If long, channel-like structures are required for spars or stiffeners, they go through a process called 'pultrusion', wherein pre-preg tape is pulled through a heated die (former) to produce the required shape.

By arranging the fibres of the composite material in particular directions, the strength or load-bearing capabilities of the resultant component can be tailored to fit the particular stresses it will experience. A good example is the forward swept wing (FSW) of the X-29 experimental aircraft. In the past, where FSWs have been tried out (as in the Junkers Ju 287 of 1944 and the HFB.320 Hansa Jet of 1964), they have been of metal construction and thicker and stiffer than equivalent swept-back wings because they are subjected to a phenomenon called 'structural divergence'. When a

metallic FSW aircraft experiences stress in flight, the wing bend causes the angle of attack (AOA) and, hence, the lift on the outer wing section to be increased. This, in turn, increases the loads on the aircraft and causes further bending and twisting of the wings. As the speed increases, these forces magnify and, eventually, exceed the strength of the wing.

To compensate for this 'structural divergence', a metal FSW had to be strengthened to a point where a weight penalty was incurred, negating any aerodynamic benefit, but the advent of graphite epoxy composites allows an FSW to be tailored to eliminate twisting when the wing bends. The X-29's wing, which is of a thin, supercritical aerofoil section less than 5 per cent thick, consists of an aluminium sub-frame with a titanium leading edge. To this sub-frame, encompassing both wings and the carry-through section, is bolted a graphite epoxy skin, built up in layers by hand, of between one-eighth and four-fifths of an inch thick. The wing skin has a glass fibre barrier to it and features a variable-camber trailing edge, making it a partial mission-adaptive wing.

Where structures are required to exhibit strength but have no need to contain internal features, like the cockpit, weapons and avionics bays, undercarriage assemblies, fuel tanks or cells, an alternative method to the use of stringers is adopted to provide this strength. Lifted straight from Mother Nature, honeycomb is a structural miracle. The essence of honeycomb is a flexible slab of vertical hexagonal passages made of a light fibre material, such as DuPont's Nomex, bonded together. All that is missing is the wax and honey. This slab of material is then cut to the shape required and load-bearing skins, of either composite or alloy metal,

◄ The use of computer-aided design (CAD) is now commonplace in aircraft drawing offices. This system is looking at the European Fighter Aircraft. (MBB/DASA)

► This early 1983 photograph shows the construction of the carbon fibre wing of the Grumman X-29 (FSW) design. (Grumman)

◄ Using the computer-aided design and manufacture (CADAM) facilities now available, models of the designer's creations can be made in relatively short times by the use of stereolithography. This technique takes the information from the CADAM program and makes a more accurate model than is possible with conventional methods employing meticulous handcrafting. (Lockheed)

◄
The X-29 FSW aircraft on an early test flight. The data gathered from the X-29 are being fed into future projects within the United States. (Grumman)

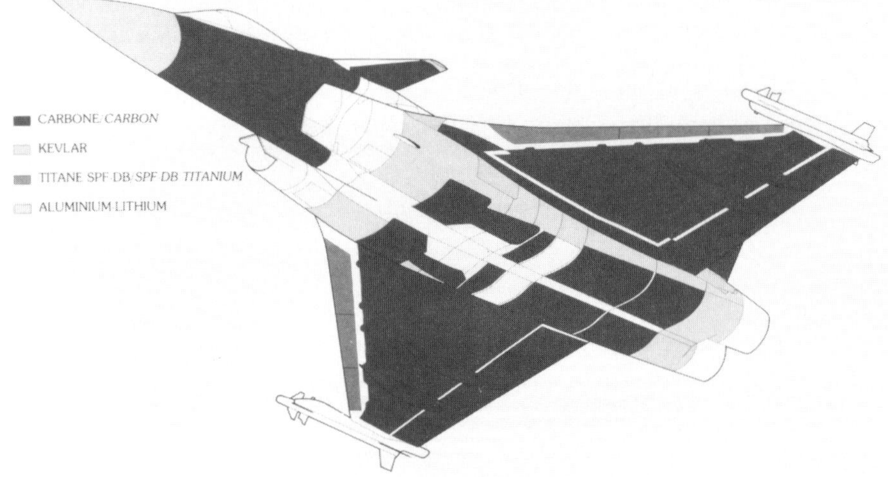

◄
A diagram showing the distribution of composite materials on the French Rafale fighter design. (Dassault/Aviaplans)

►
This view of the BAe/McDonnell Douglas Harrier GR.5 (alias AV-8B) before painting shows the high proportion of carbon fibre composite material (all the black parts) used in its construction. (BAe Military Aircraft)

are bonded top and bottom of the shaped slab. Honeycomb is already in widespread use and, where the skins are composite, it is a readily available RAS.

Two examples of the use of composites on aircraft already in service and which saw action during the Gulf War are seen in the F/A-18 Hornet and the AV-8B Harrier II. Some 10 per cent of the Hornet's structural weight is carbon epoxy material, while composites (of varying types) account for 26 per cent of the Harrier II's empty weight. As indicated above, helicopter rotor blades are now being made with composites, and many in-service types are being retrofitted with composite rotors. The reduction in take-off weight allowed by the use of composites, combined with a trend to smaller wing areas, is predicted to reduce the fuel consumption of a combat aircraft by about one-third. In the future, the use of such materials will rise to some 40 per cent of the aircraft's structure.

The most recent composite material to come on to the market is known as thermoplastic, typified by PEEK (Poly Ether Ether Ketone) and developed by ICI Advanced Materials in the mid-1980s. Thermoplastic parts are produced by moulding molten resins with reinforcing fibres under high pressure. The material is highly damage-resistant and its strength is less affected by the temperatures which prevail on the structures of high-performance aircraft. Such thermoplastics lend themselves to traditional mass-production methods such as injection-moulding and vacuum-forming. Earlier composites must be kept at high temperatures and pressures for a long time during their manufacture, so the process is time-consuming. Additionally, it is much easier to repair or re-form thermoplastic parts in the event of manufacturing faults or subsequent damage. Apart from the use of thermoplastics in aircraft or helicopter components, the production characteristics of these materials open up the possibility of manufacturing unmanned air vehicles (i.e. RPVs and drones) and missile airframes more economically.

It is fair to say that the use of composite materials in aircraft construction is now firmly established. The current US stealth programmes and the RAH-66 Com-

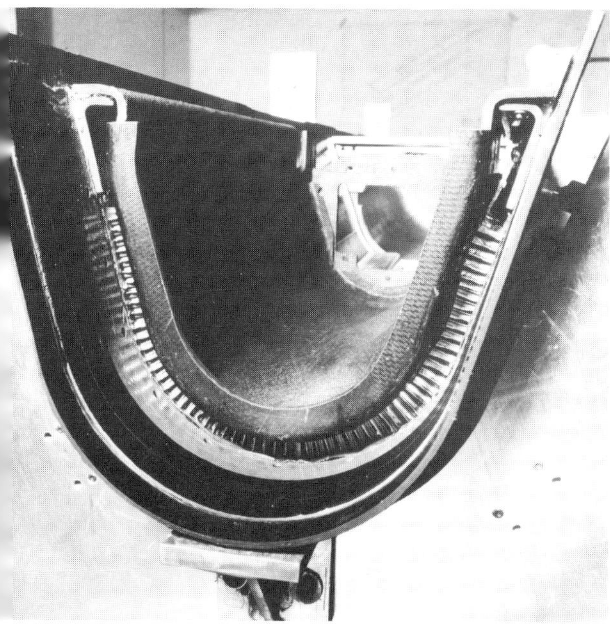

anche helicopter use high proportions, as do the JAS.39 Gripen, the EFA and the Rafale. However, the technology is still developing, and some esoteric applications are being found for the material. 'Smart skins' and other structures, for example, are under investigation. These would consist of composite structures with antennae or sensors embedded within the material during manufacture. Internal glass fibres could be used as stress sensors for the aircraft maintenance crews, while fibre-optic cables embedded in the structure could be used to transmit FBL signals through the airframe. Alternatively, metal or carbon wires could act as aerials or antennae for communications, electronic warfare or radar systems. Work is also being conducted in the United States on what are known as 'metal matrix' composites. These combine metallic reinforcing structures with fibre composites. An associated technology involves carbon-carbon composites, which retain their strength at extremely high temperatures.

As has been indicated, composites have not yet totally taken over from metal in the construction of aircraft. On-going work seeks to develop lighter and stronger alloys, as well as refining the use of titanium. One such promising material is aluminium-lithium (AlLi). This is some 9 per cent lighter and 5 per cent stronger than the more traditional aluminium alloys, with AlLi containing 2.6 per cent of lithium by weight or 16 per cent by volume. The McDonnell Douglas F-15S/MTD (STOL/Maneuvering Technology Demonstrator) being evaluated under contract to the USAF's Wright Aeronautical Laboratories includes two large AlLi structural panels on the upper wing skin. These AlLi skin panels are expected to increase performance significantly, while their extra strength will enhance the aircraft's capability for extreme manœuvring.

While metals technology has been advancing, so have metals manufacturing techniques. For some ten years, British Aerospace has been developing a technique known as 'superplastic forming', which is now used in the production of metal parts. The technique

◀ **During the 1991 Paris Air Show, Brunswick Defense of the US revealed that it is working with a new, very high temperature polymide material – known as EXP-1 by Brunswick and as the DCL series by the Daychem Laboratories where it was invented – that operates in the 800°F temperature range, has excellent electrical properties and exhibits great toughness. It is seen here being used in the mould of a fuselage section of the 'Have Dash II' air-to-air missile technology demonstrator being built for Loral Aeronutronics. (Brunswick Defense)**

◀
Some advanced composite materials, notably thermoplastic-resin composites, need to be cured in giant autoclaves, as illustrated here. (Lockheed)

involves heating metals to a temperature of about one-half that of their melting point and then distorting them in a mould under pressure. In titanium, for example, this temperature is between 800 and 925°C and for any temperature within this range the amount of deformation that can be achieved without failure is very precise. According to BAe, by carefully controlling the temperature, pressure and strain rate, this technique can achieve elongations of up to 1,000 per cent.

In conjunction with superplastic forming, BAe has also been working on diffusion bonding. This involves bringing two sheets of metal almost up to melting point and then bringing them together under pressure. The close contact between the two sheets of metal will allow them to bond together because of the diffusion of atoms across the boundary between the two. By using both techniques together (known by the acronym SPF/DB – SuperPlastic Forming/Diffusion Bonding), components can be produced in less time and with far fewer parts than by using traditional metalworking techniques.

These techniques are already in use for the construction of parts for Tornado and EFA. On Tornado, a heat-exchange duct is produced by SPF/DB, while the EFA canards are made from SPF/DB titanium. The latter have an internal structure similar to corregated card-

◀
When working with advanced materials, the use of clean-room facilities is important; this example shows the facility at BAe's military aircraft plant at Salmesbury in Lancashire. Note the autoclave in the upper right of the picture. (BAe Military Aircraft)

▶ A new wing skin, made of aluminium-lithium, is lowered on to the wing of an F-15 fighter in 1986. This was one of the first flight applications of the new alloy. (McDonnell Douglas)

board, with the skins moulded to a complex aerofoil section, while superplastic-formed AlLi is used to produce the two pressure bulkheads and drag-beams (the main load-bearing components to which the canards are attached) for the aircraft's forward fuselage. By using these SPF/DB techniques, it is estimated that cost savings of between 20 and 40 per cent can be achieved. When considering that some 10–15 per cent of components in a modern fighter like EFA can be made using this process, the overall cost benefits are obvious.

Propulsion

The advances in materials technology are having a major impact on propulsion, the vital aerospace technology. In aviation books, more often than not, powerplants tend to be ignored or, at best, only mentioned in passing. Yet without engines, any aircraft is just so much junk metal and plastic sitting on an airfield awaiting the arrival of the aerospace equivalent of Steptoe and Son.

Propulsion engineers are constantly seeking ways to reduce the weight and the fuel consumption of their engines, while increasing the power they deliver. Additionally, the recent trend is also to improve the reliability of the powerplant and its ease of maintenance and to reduce its running costs. These factors are now *de rigeur* when considering the choice of engine for any military aircraft, as planners tend to look at the overall cost of ownership of any aircraft or engine, taking into account not only its acquisition cost but also the life-cycle costs (i.e. spare parts, maintenance and fuel).

Perhaps the most significant advances in propulsion technology have been in the fabrication of turbine blades for engines. These relatively small but vital components are subjected to very high temperatures and stresses but must continue to function at high revolutions in confined spaces. To meet these harsh conditions, the durability and strength of the turbine blade have been improved by inducing the metal crystals to solidify in long, directional arrangements, tailored to meet the stresses of the operational environment. Beyond the directional crystal blade, the most recent development is the single-crystal blade. Here the blade is formed from one very large metal crystal. By eliminating the boundaries between crystals, the resulting structure is much more robust and resistant to oxidation and corrosion. As a result, the life of such blades is estimated to be five times that of earlier blades.

In order to improve the durability of and the thermal insulation required by some turbine blades, ceramic coatings can be applied. Additionally, composite materials based on metal matrix and carbon-carbon structures are also likely to be incorporated in future powerplants. Current and future engines are now being designed on CAD equipment and this has proved to be a key factor in their development. CAD has allowed the design of new, three-dimensional turbine blades, not unlike marine propellers or early airscrews, which are shorter and have more twist than the traditional blade. These 3-D blades are extremely efficient and less susceptible to damage; they also have improved reliability and reduce engine weight by requiring a smaller number per fan.

Another new feature of military powerplants is the increased use of electronic, full-authority, digital engine controls (FADEC). These are able, in effect, constantly to 'tune' the engine to ensure that it automati-

4000 CYCLE INSPECTION, 8000 CYCLE LIFE

Achieved through advanced materials

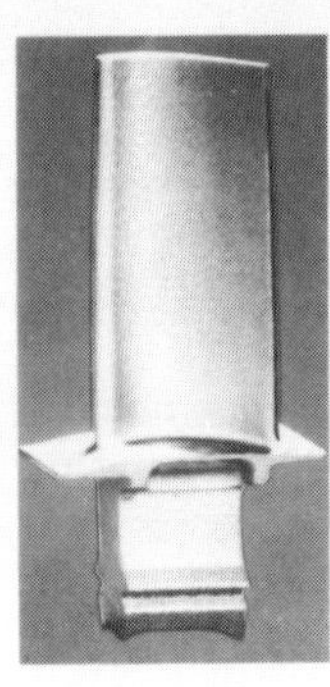

◄ **The use of improved materials is also assisting engine manufacturers. This photograph shows three engine fan blades made using the differing metallic techniques, which offer improved life and reduced inspection requirements. (Pratt & Whitney)**

cally runs as efficiently as possible. They are particularly useful where the engine exhausts have a thrust-vectoring facility, as in the Rolls-Royce Pegasus series of engines for the Harrier family.

Of course, the most important current challenge for propulsion engineers has been the development of engines for the Advanced Tactical Fighter in the United States. Any discussion of recent developments in aircraft propulsion must include the YF119 and YF120 engine prototypes, both of which have utility in a number of advanced aircraft designs. As noted earlier, two manufacturers competed for this prestigious award and, in the event, the Pratt & Whitney (P&W) YF119 was selected for production. It is enlightening to record, however, such details as have been released concerning these two projects, as they do represent the state of the art.

At the start of the competition, the USAF identified the characteristics of capabilities of the ATF powerplant: 'The ATF engines will propel the ATF at supersonic cruise speeds without using afterburners – a capability known as "supercruise". ATF engines will have two-dimensional convergent/divergent exhaust nozzles for unprecedented aircraft maneuverability. Advanced composite materials contribute to great strength and durability to the engines, with minimum weight penalty – crucial to the high thrust-to-weight ratio needed for supercruise.' Both prototype engines developed for testing under the ATF programme were in the 35,000lb (157.5kN) class.

Pratt & Whitney began the development of their YF119 turbofan engine in 1983, under a dem/val programme sponsored by the US Air Force Aeronautical Systems Division. A year later the initial development saw the design of component rigs and model tests, and by 1985 the demonstrator design and fabrication of component rigs were complete and testing had been initiated. During 1987–89 additional component core and engine testing were conducted prior to the flight testing of prototype engines, which began in August 1990.

Among the characteristics of the YF119 which have been identified by P&W are: 'Supersonic Persistence', which the company defines as 'the ability to fly at supersonic speeds for extended periods without using afterburner'; improved supportability; the use of an 'exhaust nozzle with thrust-directing features' to provide improved in-flight manœuvrability; and the expectation of 'unsurpassed combat performance, operability and durability at a lower life-cycle cost for the customer'. The YF119 was the first of the two competing engines to fly, powering the YF-23A on its maiden flight on 27 August 1990. The YF-23A, however, did not include the two-dimensional thrust-vectoring facility featured in the YF-22A. Little technical information is available at present, with P&W confining a technical description of its configuration to '...a low by-pass ratio, augmented turbofan with two counter-rotating, single-stage, HP and LP turbines'. Speaking with the author at the 1991 Paris Salon, John P. Balaguer, President of P&W's Government Engines and Space Propulsion Units, noted several areas of the YF119 programme where technology was verified in the prototype flight programme. These included advanced materials 'such as a high temperature turbine alloy and use of composites; integrally-bladed rotors; advanced aerodynamics, controlled by next-generation, full-authority digital electronic fuel control; high temperature turbine technology, using single-crystal materials and cooling techniques; and improved external plumbing and wiring'.

The GE YF120 has been flying since 29 September 1990, first on the YF-22A. During the competition, GE noted that it had successfully demonstrated variable-cycle technology, which 'enables the YF120 engines to operate like a conventional turbojet at supersonic speed, while demonstrating the characteristics of a more fuel-efficient turbofan at subsonic cruise speeds'. Another aspect of the engine was that it was constructed with 'improved materials and 40 per cent fewer parts than the [GE] F110 fighter jet engine'. In the YF120, which is a two-shaft design with the number of rotating stages reduced to 'the absolute minimum', it is understood that the high-pressure (HP) and low-pressure (LP) turbines are contra-rotating, single-stage components, with a single-stage fan (compared with three on the company's F110 engine). The use of bladed-discs ('blisks') or integrated bladed rotors has been incorporated in the design. The engine configuration uses a variable by-pass cycle (sometimes known as 'variable-cycle'), based on GE experience from a current study on high-speed commercial transport propulsion with Boeing, McDonnell Douglas and NASA. This technology involves manipulating by-pass air to enable the engine to operate like a conventional turbojet at supersonic speeds and like a more efficient turbofan at subsonic cruise speeds.

While both the YF119 and YF120 feature two-dimensional thrust-vectoring, it was only applied on the YF-22A prototype. Although some reports indicated problems with the YF120's exhaust section (i.e. the thrust-vectoring), GE denied the problem, stating that the engine has met all the requirements during ground test.

▶ This simple diagram illustrates the concept of 'supercruise' as applied to the GE YF120 turbofan. Although unsuccessful in the US ATF evaluation, the concept is still valid for the future. (General Electric)

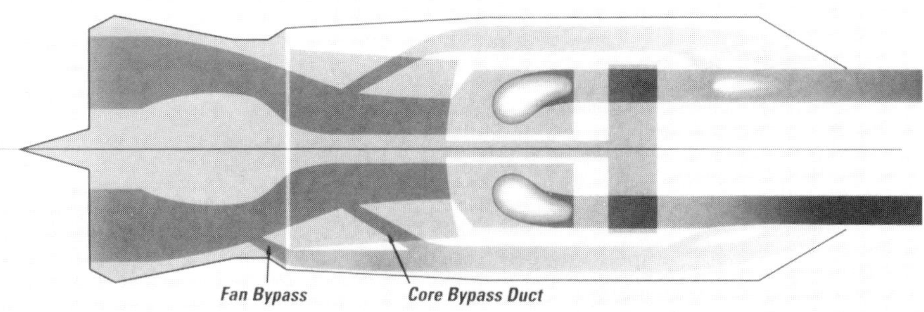

Although the history of co-operation on common aircraft between the US Navy and the USAF has not always been smooth (see previous chapter), success with common components is a little more obvious. A US General Accounting Office reports that 'The services have had more success with common use of major components such as engines, weapons, and avionics equipment.' Examples of this joint-service co-operation in aircraft engine programmes can be seen in the GE J79 engine, which was adopted for the USAF F-104 as well as for both the USAF and the USN versions of the F-4 Phantom. Already Pratt & Whitney are looking at a new design, the PW7000, in a programme jointly funded by the USAF and US Navy, to deliver 20,000lb of thrust for the proposed F/A-18E/F and, possibly, the AX.

While the future of many US aircraft programmes remains uncertain under the current procurement climate, there is potential for the joint-service exploitation of new aircraft engine technologies. Although P&W may have 'scooped the pool' as far as future USAF fighter aircraft are concerned, the General Electric (GE) YF120 is still available for the US Navy's AX (successor to the cancelled A-12), while the company's F110 and F404 engines still have much development life ahead of them.

Apart from the YF119 and YF120, there are two other stealth powerplants already flying in aircraft – in the F-117A and the B-2A. Both aircraft are powered by GE engines. The F404-GE-F1D2, which powers the F-117A, is a non-afterburning version of the -400 model powering the F/A-18. Development of the -F1D2 model began in 1980, and it first flew in the F-117A in June 1981. The B-2A is powered by the F118-GE-100, a non-afterburning derivative of the company's F101/F110 engine, rated at 19,000lb s.t. It uses new long-chord fan technology with a compressor and turbine the same as those in the F110. It has a three-stage fan with variable inlet guide vanes, a one-stage HP turbine and a two-stage LP turbine. First flown in the B-2 in July 1989, it has now accumulated in excess of 6,000 test hours.

Beyond the F110/F404 there is the F412, which was developed for the cancelled A-12. A non-afterburning derivative of the F404, it features an advanced fan and compressor, increased airflow and lower pressure ratio, a multi-hole combustor and single-crystal turbine aerofoil blades. Additionally, both the F110 and F404 series engines will benefit from GE's development work on a new Axisymmetric Vectoring Exhaust Nozzle (AVEN), which completed initial ground testing on an F110 engine in October 1990. A remote-controlled, articulated version of AVEN is planned for ground tests

◀ **Although the first development models of EFA will use the RB199 turbofan, work is progressing on the EJ200 for the aircraft. The engine is seen here in full afterburner during a ground test. (Eurojet)**

in 1992, to be followed by flight testing. The AVEN is being developed for future aircraft and for retrofit to existing fighters.

Taking a view of the world's propulsion manufacturers, there are five major companies in the United States, two each in France and Italy and one each in Sweden, West Germany and the UK, plus the dozen or so design bureaux/manufacturers in the Soviet Union. Generally speaking, although military engines are built in other countries, they tend to be designs from the major 'players', built under licence or derived from them. Several of these companies, particularly those in Europe, are involved in collaborative ventures which, in the light of current world events, seem the only sensible approach.

Across the Atlantic, two new engines are under development: the four-nation EJ200 for EFA and the M88 for the French Rafale. Eurojet Turbo GmbH – the consortium comprising MTU Munich of Germany (now part of Deutsche Aerospace), FiatAvio of Italy, ITP of Spain and Rolls-Royce of the UK – has been working on the EJ200 project since November 1988. Technology features of the engine include single-crystal turbine blades with wide-chord aerofoils, a convergent/divergent nozzle, transonic compressor design, FADEC, powder metallurgy discs, brush seals and an integrated health monitoring system.

In the 20,000lb thrust class (with afterburning or reheat), the EJ200 has logged over 650 running-hours on the first four full-scale development (FSD) engines and the first flight test engine is ready for trials. The early design verification engines have met all the technical targets set, in some cases exceeding them. All FSD engines have been run at 97 per cent of the maximum, unreheated (dry) thrust levels and 100 per cent dry thrust (13,500lb) has been demonstrated. Much of the UK contribution to EJ200 has been derived from the Rolls-Royce XG-40 advanced technology demonstrator engine, and development work on both engines is proceeding in parallel. The first EJ200 is due to fly on the third prototype EFA; the first two EFA prototypes will be powered by RB199-122 turbofans.

In France, SNECMA reports that its M88 engine had by June 1991 logged over 2,000 hours of operation. The first M88-2 flight engine, rated at 16,400lb s.t. with reheat, took off, fitted in place of the port F404-GE-400, in the Rafale-A demonstrator on 27 February 1990. On its first flight, the aircraft reached Mach 1.4 at 30,000ft without recourse to afterburner on either the M88 or F404 engine. By June 1991 the Rafale-A had logged a total of 150 flight hours. Dassault Aviation reports that the flight tests are 'being carried out at a high rate ... aiming at the qualifications of the engine before the C01 prototype's first flight, scheduled for March 1991, with two M88-2 engines'. The first pre-production Rafale, C01, flew on 19 May 1991, powered by two M88-2s, reaching Mach 1.2 and 36,000ft. By the time production Rafales are delivered, in 1996, over 5,000 hours will have been logged on the M88 engines.

For a future European fighter engine requirement, beyond both EJ200 and M88, SNECMA and Rolls-Royce have signed an agreement aimed at research into advanced materials for such an engine. This initially involves advanced composite materials for both manufacturing and repair, although specific details are not known. SNECMA is looking at an engine with a thrust-to-weight ratio of 20:1, compared with the current 10:1 ratio. SNECMA's President, Louis Gallois, told the author that such collaboration was how he saw the way ahead. 'We need alliances ... development costs are too high, markets are too difficult to go it alone,' he said. On the future of the M88 and the Rafale fighter, he noted that 'Rafale is a good aircraft for peace', predicting export sales in the late 1990s to countries wishing to replace Mirage F1s and older US aircraft.

Future engine development from SNECMA is taking several forms. Already the company has plans to develop a variant of the M88 with a thrust of 9 tonnes by changing the low-pressure parts of the engine. Another design, the MCV-99, will be a variable-cycle engine with military uses as well as application to a civil supersonic transport. Beyond these developments, SNECMA is looking to materials and technology to increase the temperatures in the engine (and hence the compression ratios), to lighten the engine structure and to improve further the fuel consumption. According to the VP for military engines, Jean Bonnet, speaking with the author at Le Bourget in June 1991, 'We have to think of [two-dimensional] vectored thrust, to be ready when the French Air Force need it ... we have taken no decision up to now.' This, he suggested, was part of a current programme within SNECMA which is looking at customer requirements rather than engineer's 'wish lists'.

Of course, collaboration is not new, either to the airframe or engine sides of the industry. The tri-national Tornado is powered by a tri-national engine, the RB199, rated at 16,000lb with reheat. This was developed and is produced by Turbo-Union, a consortium comprising MTU of Germany, Fiat Aviazione of Italy and Rolls-Royce of the UK. In order to meet the many and varied requirements of the Multi-Role Combat Aircraft (as Tornado was originally known), this three-spool turbofan offers low fuel consumption for long-range dry cruise and almost 100 per cent reheat for combat manœuvring and supersonic acceleration. A particular feature of the RB199 on the Tornado is its integral thrust reverser system, which enhances the aircraft's short-field landing performance.

Three main versions of the RB199 exist: the Mk. 103, which powers the IDS variant of Tornado, the Mk. 104 of the Tornado F.3 and the Mk. 105 for the German-developed Tornado ECR. The Mk. 103 engine has proved itself very reliable, specifically in tolerance to FOD (foreign object digestion) and bird-strikes (an occupational hazard in the aircraft's low-level role). The Mk. 104 engine incorporates a 14in jetpipe extension, providing thrust increases up to 10 per cent and a lower specific fuel consumption. It was also the first military engine to use FADEC without a hydro-mechanical back-up system. The Mk. 105 is based on the Mk. 103 and has an increased pressure ratio and mass flow LP compressor; it also uses single-crystal HP turbine blades, offering a 10 per cent thrust increase and significant reductions in life-cycle costs. This version has seen the thrust rise to 16,800lb with reheat.

For the future, the RB199 could have a totally enhanced configuration with improved materials used in its construction. The Mk. 105 programme was a step in this direction, and future versions would feature turbine nozzle-guide vanes, improved intermediate pressure (IP) and HP compressors and single-crystal IP turbine blades. Such enhancements would offer a further 20 per cent increase in thrust and significant life-cycle cost reductions.

Meanwhile, in Sweden, Volvo Flygmotor continues its development work on the RM12 (derived from the GE F404) for the JAS.39 Gripen. The modifications to the engine involved increasing its SL performance to deliver 18,000lb s.t.; the introduction of redundant control systems features, to meet single-engine requirements; and improved bird-strike capability. During 1990–91 work was concentrated on performance and airworthiness for the flight-test programme. As with any test programme, problems will occur and the RM12's has been no exception. A sudden drop in thrust at some crucial stages of the flight envelope, known as 'thrust droop', has been resolved with a modification to the digital engine control, while a problem with cracks in the third-stage compressor fan has been solved by producing a new design. All flight-test and subsequent production engines have been modified to the new standard. Production verification tests have proved that the RM12 meets both performance and function specifications. By June 1991 over 8,000 hours of ground testing had been conducted and 100 Gripen flights had been logged.

General Electric's F404 powers the F/A-18 Hornet, 835 of which are currently in service. The F404 has also been selected as the prototype engine for a number of other projects, including the USAF's X-29 and X-31 experimental designs, the French Rafale-A demonstrator and the Indian Light Combat Aircraft, as well as for re-engining Singapore's A-4 Skyhawk fleet. Derivatives, as noted earlier, power the F-117A and B-2A. In addition, as the RM12 (see above), it is the powerplant of the JAS.39 Gripen, co-developed and built by Volvo Flygmotor. As of June 1991, 2.57 million flight hours had been logged. GE report an average unscheduled rate of 1.79 visits to the engine shop per 1,000 flight hours. The F404-GE-402 Enhanced Performance Engine, in the 17,000lb s.t. class, is now in production for export Hornets, and further improvements, to 23,000lb s.t., are planned for the F/A-18E/F versions.

GE's other main engine, the F110, powers some examples of the F-16C/D/N series (as an alternative engine option) and also the F-14B/D Tomcat, using the F110-GE-100, rated at 27,600lb with reheat, and the F110-GE-400, rated at 27,000lb, respectively. GE is also developing an increased-thrust version for the F-16C/D, the -129, under the USAF's Improved Engine Performance (IPE) programme, delivering 29,000lb s.t. with reheat. The GE IPE engine uses improved design techniques and materials and offers higher operating temperatures, speeds and pressures. These enable it to produce up to 30 per cent more thrust in some regions of the flight envelope, while retaining more than 80 per cent commonality with earlier engines. The -129 model's digital engine control has, for instance, 50 per cent fewer parts than previously but offers 'substantially improved reliability'. The -129 IPE has been selected by Japan to power that country's FS-X (an F-16 derivative) fighter into the twenty-first century.

The original powerplant for the F-16A/B and some C/D models was the P&W F100, most of which in

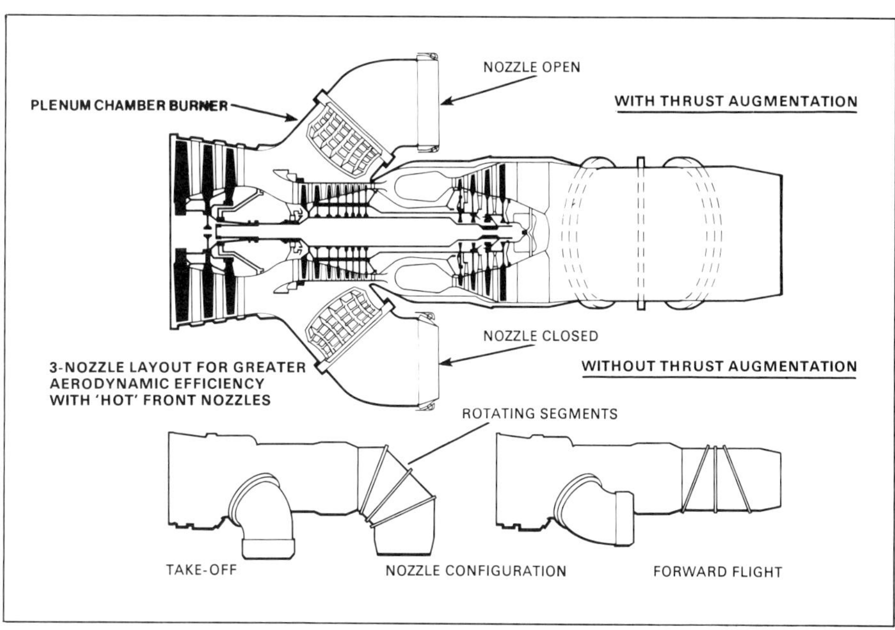

► This diagram illustrates the Rolls-Royce 'lobster-back' concept for further development of the Pegasus engine. It allows the two front nozzles to be equipped with PCB afterburning, while the rear nozzles have been replaced by a single unit for greater aerodynamic efficiency. (Rolls-Royce)

service are scheduled to be upgraded to F100-PW-220E standard, offering 23,700lb s.t.; a further upgraded engine is the -220P model, rated at 27,000lb s.t. The company recently noted that there is 'a strong international market for engine upgrades, kits and follow-on buys'. Singapore has indicated an interest in acquiring additional F-16s to add to the eight the country already has in service, which are powered by -220 engines. P&W is offering the -220 or the -229 version, rated at 29,000lb s.t., developed under the USAF IPE programme, for these aircraft. Among its features are an improved compressor and float-wall combustor. The -229 engine is lighter than earlier versions and uses a significantly smaller inlet, which helps to reduce aircraft drag and increases installed thrust.

The F100 also powers the F-15, and the company is discussing with Japan the possibility of replacing the -100s in Japanese F-15Js with the -220E. Israel has already used -220E upgrade kits to retrofit F100 engines in both its F-15 and F-16 fleets. The F100s for the F-15J are built under licence in Japan by Ishikawajima-Harima Heavy Industries. Brazil is also seen as a market for a non-afterburning, low by-pass derivative of the F100, known as the PW1115. According to P&W the company is 'negotiating with Brazil for follow-on buys of its AMX fighter to be powered by the PW1115'. P&W sees the engine as offering 'a means to improve aircraft performance and stimulate export business for Brazil'.

An engine with a less public profile is the Garrett TFE1042 70, two of which power Taiwan's AIDC Ching-Kuo indigenous defence fighter. This fully modular turbofan, rated at 8,350lb s.t. with reheat, has been under development since 1982 and the company claims that it is 'the most reliable and efficient [engine] in this power class'. It is derived from the civil TFE731, and a three-phase plan exists for the engine to grow to a maximum augmented thrust of 14,000lb s.t.

Earlier in this section, some mention was made of vectored-thrust propulsion. The major success in this area is the Rolls-Royce Pegasus series. This four-nozzle turbofan engine powers all variants of the Harrier series of fighters. The current version, the Pegasus 11-61, rated at 23,800lb s.t., is set to power the Harrier II Plus version for the US Marine Corps and the Spanish and Italian Navies.

The development of a supersonic Pegasus engine for an advanced short take-off, vertical landing (ASTOVL) fighter, using plenum chamber burning (PCB) has been considered. Although the project has not enjoyed a sustained funding level, both British Aerospace and Rolls-Royce have kept the idea of supersonic STOVL alive. In 1982, the two companies assembled a Harrier airframe from parts of two RAF aircraft written off in

◄ This photograph shows the testing of PCB in a Pegasus fitted to a test Harrier in the test-rig at P&EE, Shoeburyness, Essex. Note the 'toed-in' nature of the two forward nozzles. (Rolls-Royce)

▼ An application of the 'lobster-back' concept appears to have been made by the Soviet Union in its Yak-141 successor to the Yak-38. This wind tunnel model of the Yak-141 was displayed at Le Bourget in 1991, while journalists were shown a video of the test flights of a prototype aircraft. (Author)

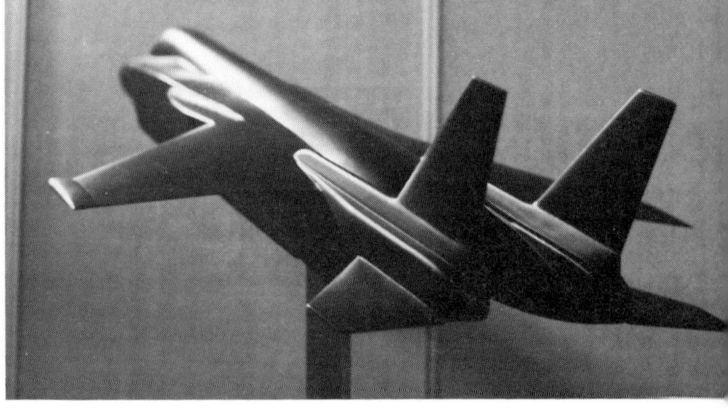

crashes, installing a Pegasus 2 engine with PCB on the forward two nozzles and mounting it beneath a gantry at a remote UK MoD facility at Shoeburyness. Since then, positive investigations into a supersonic capability for the Harrier family have been made. Valuable data were gleaned concerning higher temperatures affecting the ground surface beneath the aircraft. Put simply, while a prepared surface, (i.e. a concrete or metal vertical-landing pad) could cope with such temperatures, a grass strip such as is used by the current RAF Harrier force could not be used. Thus a supersonic Harrier derivative with PCB would not be as operationally flexible as the present aircraft: its landings would *have* to be made on a prepared surface of some description. Work is now being conducted on the airframe equipped with the current Pegasus 11 with PCB, repeating the earlier trials but providing data applicable to the higher mass and temperatures associated with this version of the engine. The work has reached a state in both companies such that, if the funding were made available, a flying demonstrator could be in the air by the end of this decade.

Despite past objections to supersonic STOVL, the US Marine Corps still foresees a need for such an aircraft. However, the emphasis has now changed slightly, and a supersonic capability on a vectored-thrust engine is not necessarily the only solution to the problem. The term 'ASTOVL' is used to describe all the efforts to move beyond Harrier. The breakthrough came in January 1986 when the US Department of Defense, NASA and the UK Ministry of Defence signed a Memorandum of Understanding to collaborate on studies to identify the next generation of ASTOVL aircraft. Using both private-venture capital and government funding for the studies, four possible configurations have emerged.

The first is our old friend, Advanced Vectored-Thrust, using the next generation of Pegasus engine with PCB. The second is the Remote Augmented Lift System (RALS), which seeks to position the nozzles of the engine further away from the aircraft's centre of gravity. Third is the Tandem Fan option, which uses a variable-cycle turbofan engine with an elongated shaft between the two fans. Inside this elongated casing is a valve which directs the airflow through different nozzles, dependent on the aircraft's mode of flight. For take-off and landing, the valve closes and directs air through the forward, vectored nozzles while, simultaneously, auxiliary air intakes on the upper fuselage surface open to draw air into the rear portion of the chamber, to be 'processed' through the second fan into the rear vectored nozzles. In conventional forward flight, the auxiliary intakes are closed and the valve is opened to allow the exhaust to pass through the rear nozzle(s), enabling the engine to operate as a conventional turbofan, with reheat if required. While being an attractive solution, it is complex and heavy. The final option is known as Ejection Augmented Lift, which has been likened to a venetian blind mounted on the aircraft wing. Air is taken from the engine and fed into a series of thin nozzles, known as ejectors, in the wing structure which combine to exhaust high-pressure air. Extra air can be introduced into these wing ejectors to augment the engine exhaust for take-off and landing. In forward flight, the ejectors are folded into the wing to reduce drag and the engine airflow is directed into a convention rear nozzle, where reheat for supersonic capability is available. This configuration is useful in that it can be adapted to an existing powerplant with the minimum of modification to the engine itself. However, the ejectors are susceptible to damage and use up valuable wing space, which would otherwise carry weapons.

These configurations were investigated by several companies on both sides of the Atlantic: BAe, MACAIR, Pratt & Whitney and Rolls-Royce have looked at Advanced Vectored-Thrust, Grumman at RALS, Lockheed ASC at the Tandem Fan and General Dynamics at the Ejection Augementation system. The terms of the MoU called for joint R&D only and leave each nation to develop an individual concept to suit its own national requirements. A long-term Technical Collaboration Agreement between Rolls-Royce and Pratt & Whitney to co-operate in the study and concept evaluation of an engine for STOVL application was signed in February 1988. This could still lead to the follow-on design and development of a demonstrator engine for flight-testing in the mid-1990s.

The Soviet Navy has a limited vectored-thrust capability with its 15,300lb Tumansky R-27V-300 turbojet installed in the Yak-38 'Forger' VTOL fighter, exhausting through two vectoring side nozzles; the other end of the VTOL engine combination consists of two Koliesov/Rybinsk RD-36-35VFR lift jets, each delivering 6,725lb of thrust. A similar approach has been adopted for the 'Forger's' successor, the Yak-141 'Freestyle', unveiled in model form at Le Bourget in 1991. The two lift jets behind the cockpit are retained, but the R-27V vectored-thrust cruise engine is replaced by an R-79 engine mounted between two tailbooms, each carrying a fin. This engine is able to vector its thrust through 90 degrees from the horizontal to the vertical. No further details are available at this stage.

The use of vectored-thrust for non-STOVL aircraft is to enable shorter landings and take-offs to be made; additionally, it can be used to improve manœuvrability in air combat. Initially 'discovered' by US Marine pilots, the use of vectored-thrust in forward flight (or 'viffing') has led to the investigation of two-dimensional vectored-thrust in more conventional aircraft – the YF-22/YF119 combination has already been mentioned. Under contract to the USAF's Wright Aeronautical Laboratories, an F-15B Eagle has been modified by McDonnell Douglas as a STOL/Maneuvering Technology Demonstrator (S/MTD). Controllable canards have been mounted on the forward upper engine intake structure, while the P&W F100 engines have been fitted with 2-D thrust-vectoring nozzles. Initial results for the use of the thrust-vectoring have been promising.

The most advanced programme to use 2-D thrust-vectoring is the Rockwell International/MBB X-31 developed for the Enhanced Fighter Maneuverability (EFM) programme. Designed to investigate aircraft performance at high angles of attack (AoA), the GE F404 powerplant has been fitted with three 'paddle' blades for thrust-vectoring. The first of two X-31s flew in March 1990, and results from this programme are expected to be fed into the F-22 ATF and other advanced projects. However, as to what these and other demonstrator aircraft might look like is a closely guarded secret. The designers themselves probably do not even know yet, as there are many other factors to be introduced into the equation beyond the airframe/engine combination. What, for example, will be the impact of stealth? Although the logical solution might be the evolutionary path of Advanced Vectored-Thrust, another, revolutionary, concept could show the way forward just as vectored-thrust itself did in the early 1960s. What does appear certain is that STOVL aircraft do have a future.

At this stage, one should also mention the engines being developed for the light strike/trainer class of air-

◀
The F-15 STOL Maneuver Technology Demonstrator (S/MTD) is seen here in flight. Note the two-dimensional nozzles attached to the exhausts of the F100 turbofans. (MACAIR)

craft. While not being at the forefront of high performance, they do exhibit improved fuel consumption and improved reliability and maintainability. The market is still an attractive one in which to participate – witness the recent orders from Oman and Malaysia for Hawks (both the trainer and single-seat 200-series light fighter variants in each case), which testify to the stability of this particular part of the market, and to its competitiveness.

The Hawk is powered by another collaborative venture, the Rolls-Royce/Turboméca Adour turbofan in its non-afterburning configuration. Developed for the Anglo-French Jaguar programme, the original engine was raised to a thrust level of 8,400lb s.t. with reheat. The Hawk applications have seen the unaugmented thrust level raised to 5,875lb s.t. with the Adour Mk. 871, which powers the single-seat Hawk 200. Apart from Hawk exports around the world, including to the United States (as the T-45 Goshawk), the Adour was adapted for the Mitsubishi F-1 fighter/close support and T-2 trainer aircraft programmes in Japan, where it was built under licence there by Ishikawajima-Harina Heavy Industries. Adours for Indian Jaguars and Finnish Hawks have also been built under licence in the respective countries.

Slightly down the scale, but still in the same market, is the Garrett TFE731 which powers Spain's CASA 101 and Argentina's FAMA IA-63 Pampa. Basically developed as a powerplant for various 'bizjets', the engine has been developed into the TFE731-5A offering higher thrust, 1,500lb s.t., and reduced noise, while retaining the low smoke characteristics. The -5A has a higher bypass ratio fan, driven by a new LP turbine.

Although virtually at the end of its development potential, the venerable Rolls-Royce Viper turbojet is in service in aircraft in 29 countries, in both civil and military aircraft. It has been built under licence in Australia (by HDHV), Italy (Piaggio), Romania, South Africa (Atlas) and Yugoslavia. In the jet trainer category, the latest customer for the Viper is New Zealand, where the 680 version will power the recently delivered Aermacchi MB.339C. For an engine that was developed as a 'throw-away' powerplant for the Jindivik target drone, it has done extremely well.

Further down the trainer powerplant scale is the turboprop engine, which is, basically, a jet engine where the drive shaft powers a propeller. Such engines offer better performance over piston engines and are good powerplants for the transitional stage of training, leading to jet aircraft like the Hawk or Alpha Jet. However, their use on combat aircraft is limited to the Turboméca Astazou XVIG, rated at 965shp, which powers Argentina's IA-58 Pucará. The turboprop is, however, widely used to power transport and maritime surveillance aircraft; the Allison T56, for example, is used on both the C-130 Hercules transport and the P-3 Orion maritime patrol and ASW aircraft. In this field, the developments of the turbofan engine, in terms of design and materials, are reflected. However, the one area of advancement not applicable to jet engines is propeller technology. Taking advantage of CAD/CAM and composite materials, the number of blades has grown from an average of four to five, six and beyond. These propellers offer improved efficiency in the cruise mode, which is where many aircraft powered by such engines spend most of their air-time.

A new turboprop in the 5,000shp class is the Allison T407, which features FADEC and IR-signature-reducing exhausts (a survivability factor also used in the stealth programmes). For its original application on the now defunct P-7 replacement for the Orion, the T407 drives a Hamilton Standard 15WF five-bladed, modular, composite propeller. Although its lead project was cancelled by the US Navy, the T407 should find other applications, not least in the expected successor, a further-developed version of the P-3. Another Allison project, the 6,150shp T406, powers the V-22 Osprey tilt-rotor aircraft, a cross between a turboprop transport and a helicopter. Among its features are FADEC and a fully self-contained oil system capable of operation in the vertical as well as horizontal mode. Being modular in concept, the T406 provides a basis for further development as turboprop, propfan or turbofan applications, should the fight for the V-22's survival fail.

Military transport and similar types also benefit from advances in commercial airliner developments, where the emphasis is on better endurance and payload capabity. The advent of commercial turbofans has been a particular boon to military transports, by reducing fuel consumption, which translates into either longer range or improved cargo weights. On a commercial turbofan, the front turbine is larger than the others and acts as a large propeller inside a duct. This improves fuel efficiency and, incidentally, reduces engine noise and exhaust temperature. The use of the CFM56 (jointly developed by GE in the USA and SNECMA in France) on the E-3 Sentry (AWACS) aircraft has increased the time-on-station of these radar pickets by some two hours. The same engine is being retrofitted into most (over 600) of the USAF's fleet of KC-135 aerial tanker aircraft. The P&W F117-PW-100 turbofan, an uprated, military version of the PW2037 which powers some Boeing 757 airliners, is being used on the McDonnell Douglas C-17A airlifter. Single-crystal blades and FADEC are among the features of this engine.

The helicopter powerplants of today and the future are based on turboprop engine technology and are known as turboshaft engines. All the developments related to design, technology and materials have been involved in the production of such new engines as the LHTEC (a consortium of Allison and Garrett) T800 for the RAH-66 Comanche and the collaborative MTR 390 turboshaft being developed by MTU of Germany, Turboméca of France and the UK's Rolls-Royce, initially for use on the Eurocopter Tiger attack helicopter. Already the T800 has been adapted for and flown on other helicopters beyond the Comanche and, doubtless, the MTR 390 will find other airframes to power in the future.

From these glances at the present and into the future, it appears that despite an expected reduction in orders for new airframes, developments will continue. With the upsurge expected in the retrofit market, allowing improved performance and reduced costs of ownership, engine manufacturers will be far from idle, albeit with a slightly lower output than today. Bernard L. Koff, Senior Vice President for Engineering at Pratt & Whitney, commenting on the future of military propulsion, says, 'The advances in jet propulsion that have been so successfully applied in commercial aviation have come from military engines. This trend will continue as long as a viable, military aircraft propulsion initiative continues. Advanced higher efficiency, better materials, more effective cooling and combustion systems with lower emissions are representative of ongoing technologies funded by the government for military programmes with commercial applications.' He concludes, 'The road ahead is clear. It is essential to keep the "technology development fire" going in military propulsion, so the world can benefit through a continued state of military preparedness, lower-cost improved commercial travel and conservation of our liquid petroleum resource.'

New developments will undoubtedly continue but, as Louis Gallois of SNECMA has pointed out, alliances between manufacturers will also continue to flourish. The emergence of the Soviet Union on to the international scene will offer chances for further alliances, although, as Gallois noted, 'they want to shift from military to commercial engines'. Nevertheless, as in the past, as new requirements emerge, the aero engine industry will be able to respond.

For the combat aircraft of today and tomorrow, avionics – the word is a contraction of 'aircraft electronics', collectively embracing the radar, passive sensors, navigation, electronic warfare and communications – will comprise over half the cost of the aircraft. It is in this region that the technology of the 'black box' comes into its own. This chapter endeavours to explain the various areas more in terms of capability rather than detailed technology; to do otherwise would entail a volume dedicated entirely to the subject. Again, the requirements of stealth will intrude into the performance of many systems, some requiring the use of such technology in their operation, others being a means to the end of the stealth requirement.

However, before looking at the various systems themselves, a basic concept must be explained. If one can comprehend that all the previously mentioned areas are highly complex systems in their own right, it follows that the pilot and other air crew must receive the data from the various systems, correlate them, form a picture and make a decision on what to do next. Obviously, this can mean a total data overload for the air crew. Somewhere along the line there must be a way for this data to be filtered so that the pilot is presented with the information he needs, or summons through his controls in the 'glass cockpit', in a plausible order so that he can make the necessary decisions. Nowadays this is accomplished by linking all manner of individual computers on a hard-wire 'ring main' known as a databus. This can also be used to handle the flight control functions as well as the sensors and weapons management areas of control. The majority of such databuses are manufactured to, or are produced to be compatible with, NATO Military Standard 1553B (often shortened to 'MIL STD 1553B' or just referred to as a '1553B databus'). Each computer interfaced with the databus has what is known as a 'driving protocol' which allows it to address other systems computers, acting like a handshake before a conversation. Thus the pilot can call up what information he requires on his multi-function displays. For the future, fibre-optics will be used in databuses, as they can handle greater volumes of information for a given weight and volume of system. Eventually, quaduple fibre-optic databuses should become the norm. As an intermediate step, EFA is to have a twin-wire and one fibre-optic link databus (to a new standard), and, it is believed, this will be the first combat aircraft with such a system.

For the future, work is progressing towards giving this computer some form of artificial intelligence in order further to remove some of the thinking from the pilot's loop. This can save vital microseconds in combat and is known as 'situation awareness' or 'data fusion'. Such technology is already being developed for the next generation of combat aircraft such as the F-22, B-2, Rafale, Gripen and EFA. An interim stage is the so-called 'expert' system which takes sensor data and offers the pilot three choices as to the likely threat, with a, say, 90, 75 and 50 per cent probability of accuracy increase. Systems like the US 'Pilot's Associate' or the French DR 3000 are under development now.

The key to this and all future developments in avionics is in the data processing. The integrated circuits, or chips, are becoming smaller and, at the same time, more powerful – in either speed of processing or memory storage. Parallel processing is also increasing the speed of systems, to say nothing of their complexity. The effective standard in this area of processors is the Motorola 68000 series chip: look in any modern system and you will find one (or more) there somewhere. So, in the light of this comparatively simple explanation of a most complicated science, let us consider the various aspects of avionics.

Radar

Airborne radar can be split into five main categories as far as military aviation is concerned. Air interception radar and air-to-ground radar (sometimes lumped together by the general term 'fire-control radar') are used by fighters and bomber/strike aircraft respect

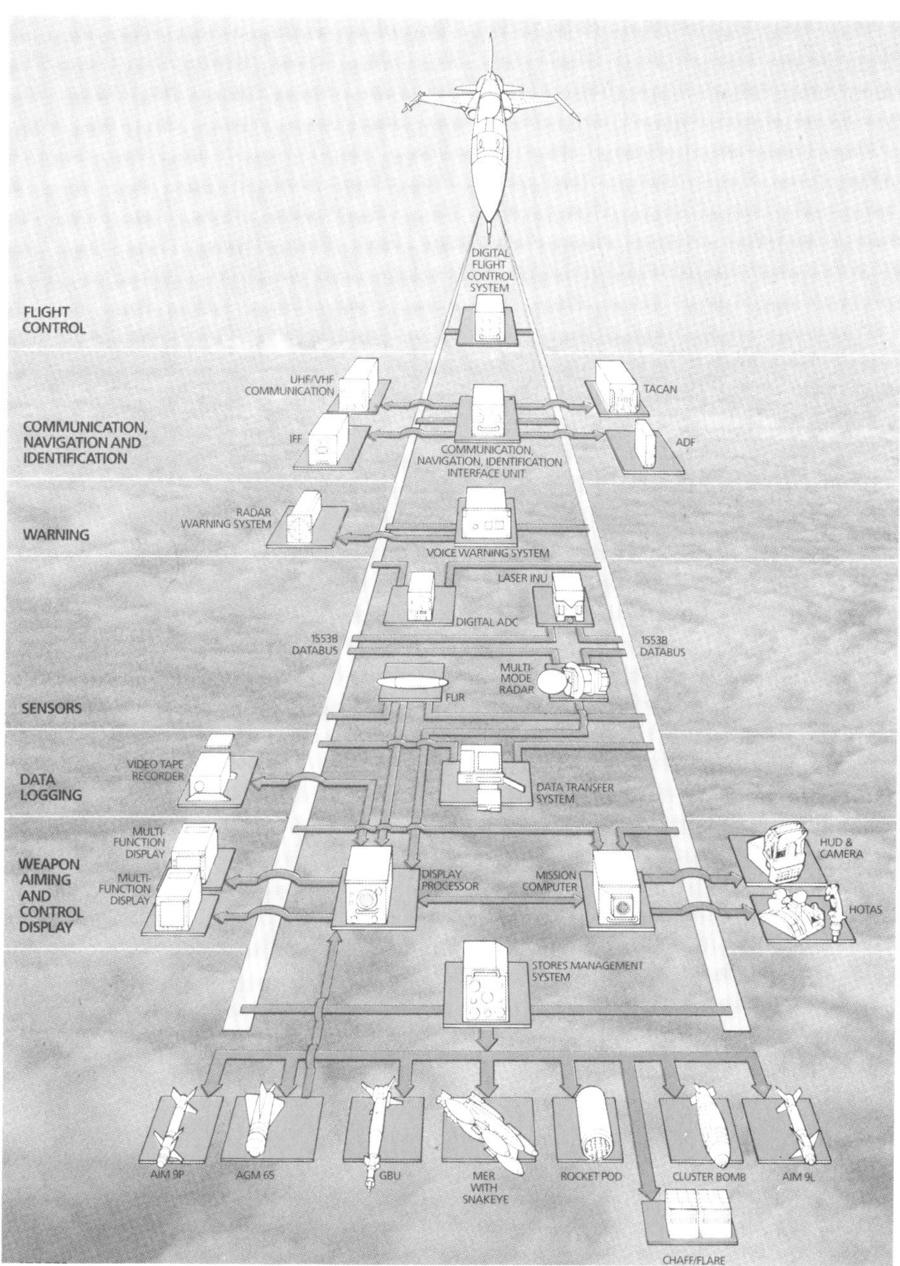

▶ This diagram illustrates the application of a 1553B databus in a combat aircraft. This specific example relates to a proposed upgrade of the F-5E fighter. (Smiths Industries)

◀ On display at Le Bourget in 1991 was this example of the radar installed in the Soviet MiG-29 'Fulcrum' fighter aircraft. Note the bulk of the 'black boxes' behind the antenna. (Author)

ively; sea surveillance and airborne early warning (AEW) radars are specialized systems; while navigational radars are used in non-combat aircraft and are virtually identical to the systems used in commercial aviation. Within the latter category, however, one can also include the specialized station-keeping radar used by some transport aircraft which have to fly in formation in order to drop paratroops. The basic component parts of all radar systems comprise an antenna with transmitter and receiver elements; a transmitter mechanism, usually in the form of a travelling wave tube (TWT) which generates raw energy which is then modulated (pulsed) to produce the signal required; a signal processor to receive the returns and then extract the target echo from the background clutter; system cooling (since all this radar energy makes the component parts very hot); a 'gating mechanism', which defines the duty cycle of the individual radar (i.e. how often it transmits and receives); and, of course, the radar display itself.

Air interception radar, as its name suggests, is used on fighters to detect and destroy enemy aircraft in the air. Obviously long range is a prime requirement and, as height extends range, a look-down capability is required. Looking down means that ground returns are also received, so these must be filtered out by the signal processor. An aid to this filtering is the use of pulse-Doppler techniques, which work on the change in frequency of the received signal engendered by the movement of the target, known as its Doppler shift. Alongside range/altitude is the simple physical fact that the larger the antenna, the better resolution the received signal has. Typical of such systems are the Hughes APG-63 and APG-70 of the F-15A/C/E, the Hughes AWG-9 and APG-73 of the F-14A/D and the GEC-Marconi AI.24 Foxhunter of the Tornado F.3.

These radars, however, all use mechanical scanning systems. Developments are progressing in the use of electronic scanning techniques. Typical of such work is the French RBE2 radar from Thomson-CSF. Put simply, a focused radar beam is generated at the back of the set, which is then fed through a mechanical 'lens'. This consists of a set of holes, each with a ferrite diode, which is used to 'bend' the beam in azimuth. This then passes through a polarizer and a second lens, which bends the beam in elevation. Thus the need for mechanical scanning is removed. This technique is known as passive electronic scanning.

The next stage in development is active scanning. Here the antenna comprises some 1,500–2,000 individual transmitter/receiver modules on a flat surface known as a phased-array. The computer circuitry and software then control the gate mechanism to allow a radar beam to be swung in both azimuth and elevation. The principal advantage is that the beam can be swung in any direction very quickly. It has the additional advantage of 'graceful degradation'. This means that should any of the modules fail, for whatever reason, then although the radar becomes less capable it

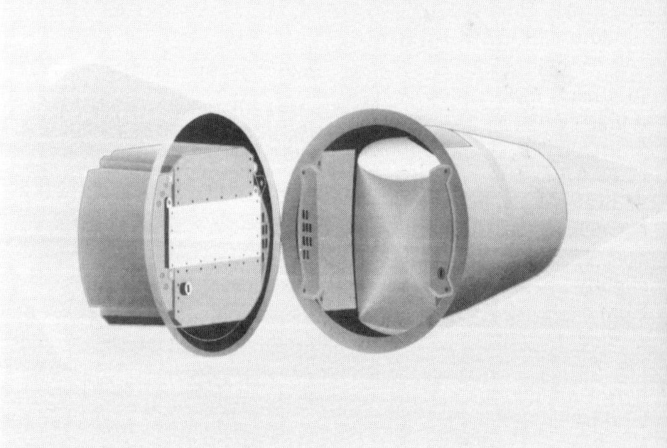

can still operate. In the passive scanning radar, should any major part (say, one of the lenses) be damaged, the whole radar goes down.

Texas Instruments and Westinghouse are working together to produce an active scanning radar for the USAF's F-22 ATF and, although the technology is proved, the driver in the development programme is the cost of each individual module in the array. In 1991 GEC-Marconi and Thomson-CSF signed an agreement to work together to develop the technologies required to produce an active array radar for the generation of fighters beyond EFA and Rafale. In all cases it is the need to place a system in production at an acceptable cost which accounts for much of the development work

◄
A mock-up of the ECR-90 radar being developed for the EFA by a four-nation consortium, led by GEC-Ferranti in the UK. A multi-mode system, it will be capable of air-to-air and air-to-ground work. (GEC-Ferranti via MBB)

►
This experimental solid-state, phased-array (SSPA) radar is being developed by Texas Instruments for the USAF's Wright Aeronautical Laboratory. The use of low-power SSPA modules makes the less reliable, mechanically scanned antennae and high-voltage transmitters a thing of the past. The engineer is holding one of the many SSPA modules. (Texas Instruments)

◄
Another multi-mode radar under development is the French RBE2 from Thomson-CSF for the Rafale. It is equivalent to the ECR-90 but will also address air-to-sea applications (requiring slightly different software from that for the air-to-ground model) as Rafale is being developed in a carrier-borne version as well as a land-based version. (Thomson-CFS)

– getting the right materials and design for a system to be affordable. At the 1991 Paris Salon the Soviet Union surprised the world when it removed the nosecone of the MiG-31 'Foxhound' interceptor displayed at the show to reveal the world's first active antenna radar. It is known as Zaslon, and the Soviets claim that it has been in service since 1983 and has proved very effective. It is credited with a range of some 120km and, they say, it is able to track up to ten targets simultaneously and engage four at once. At the time of writing, Western experts have still to make more than a qualified judgement on its performance and technology, but, if all claims are true, it is a remarkable achievement.

Today most modern radars are multi-mode systems able to be used for air defence or for offensive operations. To enable them to accomplish these latter tasks, ground-mapping facilities are built into the radar processing system: all the pilot is required to do is switch his set from air search to ground-mapping modes. While some physical modifications may be required to the radar system hardware, most of the changes to enable this function to be carried out are of a computer software nature. The success of such systems varies in that some radars are designed principally for air interception and have only a nominal ground-mapping facility; others, such as the Hughes APG-65/73 series of the F/A-18 Hornet, are true multi-mode systems.

Dedicated air-to-ground radars are used for a variety of functions, including pinpointing targets and launching air-to-ground weapons, navigation, terrain-following and terrain-avoidance (TF/TA). Today, virtually all NATO day strike/attack aircraft are equipped with inertial navigation systems (INS) – see below – but low-level bombing/strike operations at night are carried out by aircraft fitted with TF/TA radar systems. These types are few in number: the F-111 series, the F-15E, the B-1B and the Tornado IDS. As low-level radar-guided guns and SAMs are just as efficacious by night as by day, low-level operations 24 hours a day, and in all weathers, are still vital. The development of TF/TA radars have made this possible. However, by using such systems, which radiate energy, these aircraft are just as susceptible to radar-guided ground defences. The dark hours can no longer be considered a 'cloak' behind which intruding aircraft can hide.

The use of TF/TA radars is almost an act of faith on the part of the air crew flying the aircraft, yet they *are* valid, especially in conjunction with an INS. The F-111 did not enjoy a good reputation in its early service, and so the USAF took radical steps to counter this 'bad press': when any critic of the F-111 took the stage, he was invited to participate in an F-111 low-level flight to demonstrate that all was not as had been reported. The majority of the aircraft's critics were, thus, effectively silenced. Indeed, this policy drew many converts and today, whatever other criticisms can be made of the F-111, its effectiveness at low level is no longer an issue. The equipment which made the F-111 a safe low-flyer was the APQ-110 TFR (terrain-following radar), produced by Texas Instruments (TI). The TFR is a forward-looking, air-to-ground system that measures range and angle to the terrain along a flight path. That information is used by a terrain-following computer to calculate a flight vector to enable the aircraft to maintain a pre-set clearance above the terrain. TI considers itself to be the leader in such radar systems, despite the pre-eminence of such names as Emerson, General Electric, Hughes Aircraft and Westinghouse in the field of the 'sexier' fire-control radar systems which may also include ground-mapping (GM) facilities. Apart from equipping the F-111, TI supplies the TFR radar system installed in the interdictor-strike (IDS) version of the European Tornado. This is, in fact, two radar systems in one: one handles the GM requirement while the other system, with a smaller antenna mounted below the GM antenna, is for terrain-following. Curiously, it carries no current US military designation in the AN series and is known universally as the 'Tornado nose radar'.

There is no doubt in the minds of the military that such systems visibly enhance night air operations, especially as they can be coupled to the autopilot to allow automatic terrain-following. However, it must be said that, even though TFRs allow strike and attack aircraft to fly blind, low-level profiles with terrain-masking providing a defence against enemy radars, there are points in the mission profile where unmasking occurs and the emitted radar energy becomes another pointer to aircraft position ... and it can be jammed. TFR on its own is not the total answer to night air operations. Although recent developments make TFRs 'yesterday's technology', they still have a part to play within the concept of integrated night attack avionics suites. Indeed, a TFR is used in Martin Marietta's LANTIRN (Low Altitude Navigation and Targeting Infra-Red for Night) system for the F-15E and F-16C, and a multi-mode derivative, the APQ-168, has been selected for the V-22 Osprey tilt-rotor craft.

Another specialized area of radar development is in the sea surveillance role, be it for the detection of surface vessels or submarine snorkel masts. Being directed at the surface of the sea, there is much emphasis on the filtering of background clutter, which is achieved principally by software and some circuitry in the range/velocity gates. Initially developed for the anti-submarine warfare (ASW) role, such systems have also been adapted for use by less specialized aircraft under the general category of maritime patrol. Thus one can

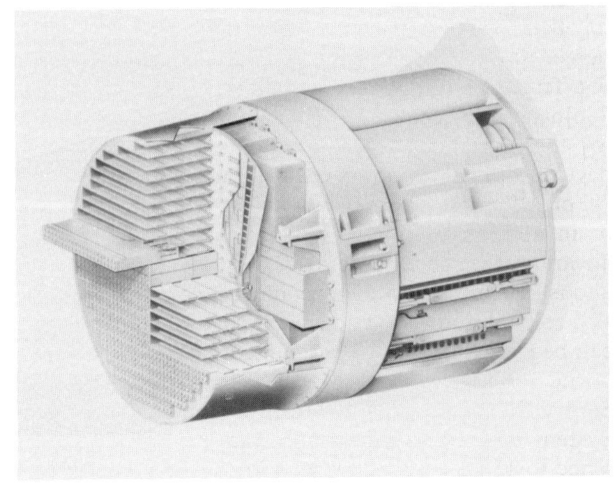

► The advent of SSPA technology and the upcoming 'smart skin' will allow radar and aircraft designers to make their systems more aerodynamically efficient by embedding the radar in the aircraft's natural geometry. These 'conformal antennae' will replace the large external radomes associated with many AEW and maritime patrol aircraft and helicopters. (Grumman)

◄▼ Europe is making advances in SSPA technology, and in mid-1991 GEC-Ferranti of the UK and Thomson-CSF of France set up a joint company to promote the enabling technologies for this type of radar. (Thomson-CSF)

find specialized long-range ASW maritime patrol aircraft equipped with such systems as the Thorn EMI Searchwater (on the Nimrod MR.2) or TI's APS-115 (on the P-3C Orion).

The use of synthetic aperture radar (SAR – not to be confused with Search and Rescue; acronyms must be used in context!) can enhance the quality and resolution of radar images. As noted earlier, the bigger the radar, the greater the resolution. SAR antennae are usually longer, so what happens is that the returns from one sweep or sector are stored until a given number of these have been recorded. They are then 'added together' in the processor to give the effect of a much bigger antenna, with the previously mentioned benefits. The best example of its application is in the two E-8 joint-STARS aircraft which were pressed into service for the 1991 Gulf War (even though they were still developmental) and achieved excellent results.

For AEW roles, a larger radar is mounted above the main airframe of the host aircraft. This has all the advantages of height and range previously mentioned and is, of course, specifically tailored for its 'eye-in-the-sky' role. An important adjunct is that the host aircraft can be used to control other combat aircraft while airborne itself. Hence the role title for the USAF's E-3 Sentry AEW aircraft is Airborne Warning and Control System (AWACS). (If the author may be allowed a sentence to make a point, AWACS is *not* the name of the aircraft itself, only its role; he has lost count of the number of times the E-3 Sentry is referred to as 'an AWACS'.)

Throughout this section, one point comes through very strongly: it is in the application of the basic laws of physics that the breakthroughs and developments occur. To accomplish these without improvements in computer processing would have been impossible. Computers come in two parts: the hardware or computer itself; and the software, the tool which drives the computer and allows it to accomplish its designated task. Until fairly recently, most computers have had their software embedded in the system, and to change any parameters meant the whole system being removed and re-input. The adoption of the Ada software language, which is almost modular, has enabled any computer-driven system, be it radar, electronic warfare, communications, etc., to be re-programmed with relative ease. For the future, common families of processors and sensor antennae are being considered, with the F-22 the first likely application.

Passive Sensors

In this context, we are considering a passive alternative to a radar; the latter is, by its very nature, an active system which radiates energy. Here we are moving into

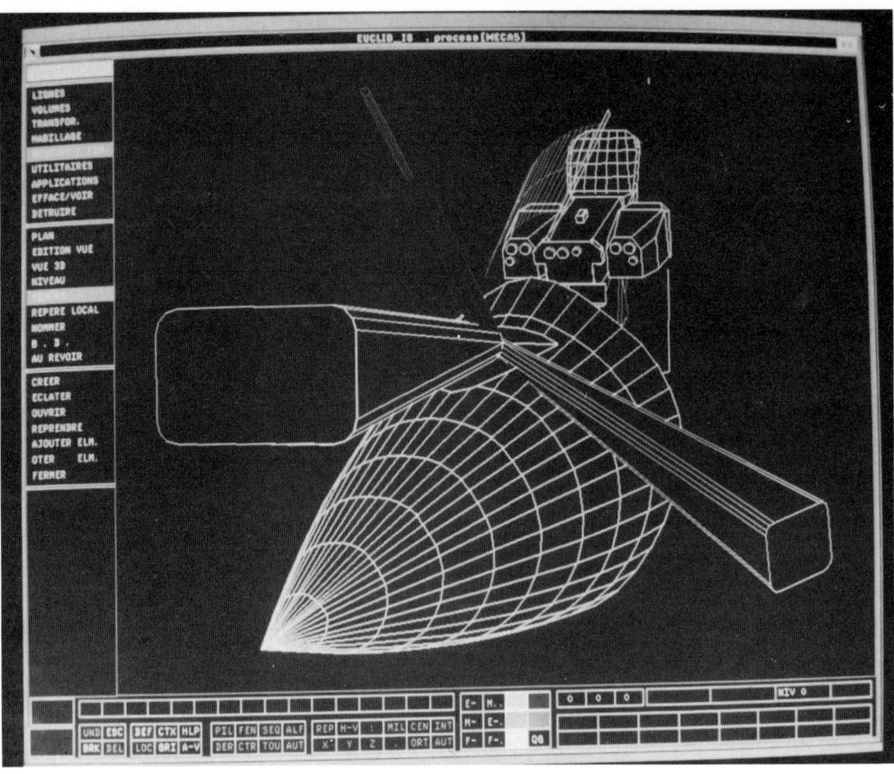

◄ The use of CAD is extending into the avionics field, as this view of the IRST project for the Rafale fighter shows. Already operational in some Soviet fighters, IRSTs are scheduled to become the major passive sensor on many combat aircraft of the next century. (Thomson-CSF)

► For larger aircraft, the heart of the weapons system is the mission avionics suite. This view of the mission system displays on board the French Atlantique 2 maritime patrol and ASW aircraft allows for data input from radar, a thermal imager and acoustic (sonobuoy) and magnetic (MAD) sensors. (Dassault/Aviaplans)

▼ This view of the EFA mock-up at Le Bourget in 1991 shows the IRST fairing to the port side of the cockpit windscreen. (Author)

the electro-optical (E-O) area of technology. For fighter aircraft, this means an infra-red search-and-track (IRST) system, although long-range television cameras are sometimes used to assist in that sometimes vital function of a visual identification.

The IRST-type system is not unknown to NATO air forces. During the 1970s, an early form of IRST from Hughes Aircraft was fitted in USAF F-101B Voodoo, F-102 Delta Dagger and F-106 Delta Dart fighters. The author understands, however, that these sets are no longer in service. The best the West can offer, at present, is the Northrop ASX-1 TISEO (Target Identification System Electro-Optical) close-circuit TV unit mounted on the leading edge of many USAF F-4E Phantoms, and its US Navy equivalent, the AXX-1 TCS (Television Camera Set) mounted in an undernose pod on the F-14 Tomcat. Both systems are only effective in clear-weather day-time operations.

Although work on IRST equipment has been under way in the West, notably by Texas Instruments with their Falcon Eye system to fit an F-16, and many other companies are now involved in parallel work, it was, perhaps, the arrival of the first MiG-29 'Fulcrums' at the 1988 Farnborough Air Show – equipped with an in-service IRST – that first brought such systems to the public's attention. This interest was reinforced a year later when the first Sukhoi Su-27 'Flankers' arrived at

the Paris Air Show. The MiG-29s had E-O sensors – an IRST system and a laser ranger, plus a fully developed helmet-mounted sight (HMS) – to complement their radar. Both the IRST and the laser ranger use Cassegrain optics: the IRST (with a reported range of 15nm) was considered to be more accurate in angular tracking than a radar and the laser ranger is far more accurate than a radar for ranging. Each system is autonomous but they are usually interlinked via the aircraft fire-control computer.

Writing in *Flight Daily*, published during the Farnborough Air Show, veteran aviation commentator Bill Gunston described how the system works. 'If we are above cloud – where we might be seconds after take-off – we may be in a clear sky and detect a target on the extraordinarily sensitive IRST. This locks-on automatically and does not lose the target. Suppose the bad guy tries to evade by diving into the clouds. IR wavelengths suddenly aren't so good. No problem, the cloud-detection sub-system realises that the IR isn't helpful and switches on the radar. Parts of it, such as the high-power transmitter, are already "warmed up" and we have a picture instantly. What's more, the target appears bang in the middle, no matter what the conditions, cued by the IRST memory. Maybe we suddenly emerge into the clear again. By this time the target can be seen visually, and it appears in the right place in the sight reticule.' The MiG chief test pilot, Valery Menitsky, talking at the Show, commented further that all that was required was 'a watching brief'. He continued: 'But it is often important to make a stealthy approach, and so you can inhibit the switch-on of the radar. Believe me, you can make a very good interception using just the two E-O systems and HMS.'

While not the pure *raison d'être* for IRST development in the West, the close-up view of the Soviets' system and their claims for its effectiveness certainly did wonders for the rate of development of such systems within Western industry. So what is an IRST? Put simply, it is a 'passive radar' which allows an aircraft so equipped to detect and track airborne targets without exposing itself by the active transmission of a radar beam. The IR spectrum is divided into three principal wavebands: the very near, which equates to

◄◄
The Thermal Imaging Airborne Laser Designator (TIALD) system was rushed into service during the Gulf War to assist the RAF with their laser designation of targets by day or night. This view shows the thermal image of a power station (not taken operationally over Iraq). Note the chimneys and storage tanks. (GEC-Ferranti)

▲►
A view of the same power station taken by TIALD's television camera. Note the boats on the river – not obvious on the thermal image. (GEC-Ferranti)

◄
A TIALD pod under a Tornado GR.1, used in trials before the two TIALD systems in existence were despatched for operational service in the Gulf. (GEC-Ferranti)

IR photography; the medium (3–5 micron) wavebands, which are sensitive to inherently 'hot' objects such as the sun or the tailpipe of a jet engine; and the long (8–13 micron) wavebands, which are sensitive to natural heat radiated against natural surroundings. The trick, so far as an IRST is concerned, is to develop a sensor which is capable of operating in dual modes – the medium and long wavebands – and a processor capable of handling the input at the necessary high speeds. It is the processor, using automatic algorithms, which turns a FLIR sensor into an IRST system. By installing an IRST on a 'non-stealth' in-service fighter, its new host is given another advantage. In time, we could well see advanced IRSTs replacing radar in interceptor fighters. Both EFA and Rafale will have IRSTs: the former's system is still (at the time of writing) open to competition, but the latter's will come from Thomson-CSF. For bomber/strike aircraft and attack/special operations helicopters, it is a forward-looking infra-red (FLIR) system. Transports, both fixed- and rotary-winged, can be fitted with FLIR, although it is usually cheaper for air forces to opt for night vision goggles (NVGs) for the air crew, unless specific operations call for the use of a FLIR. Meanwhile, NVGs (coupled with suitable lighting for the cockpit instrumentation) are fast becoming standard for all forms of combat aircraft.

We are now entering the field of night vision, the two main sensors for which are passive. A FLIR uses IR energy to present a picture not unlike a black-and-white photograph image on a cathode ray tube (CRT) like a TV screen. FLIRs have found applications in all aspects of airborne operations at night, not just the attack role. The ability to obtain a picture of the outside world, albeit in a monochrome form, has been of major importance in both passive (navigation) and offensive (targeting) modes.

The heart of any FLIR system is its thermal imaging system, and several countries have developed modular thermal imaging systems programmes to supply this vital core for a number of military applications. In France, TRT and SAT have collaborated to produce a range of such modules, while in the UK, GEC Avionics and Rank Taylor Hobson have worked together on the Thermal Imaging Common Modules (TICM) programme. The former programme has produced a system for the Atlantique 2 maritime patrol aircraft, while the latter's airborne application (in the form of TICM 2) is a night vision system for the Tornado GR.4 mid-life update, proving the desirability to match a night vision capability to both TFR- and non-radar equipped aircraft, and for night attack variants of the Harrier II. In the United States, Texas Instruments is the predominant manufacturer of FLIR systems, including those for the night attack version of the F/A-18C/D Hornet.

The application of FLIR to targeting, whether built in to the airframe or pod-mounted, is very relevant to night air attack operations, as was proved during the 1991 Gulf War. Targets could be found at night and in certain conditions of bad weather, allowing laser designation for precision-guided munitions to be used against them. We all saw the results of these strikes on our television sets nightly during the war.

Navigation

There are many systems which may be used to navigate aircraft by day and night. Believe it or not, a map and stopwatch still works, and FLIR can help. However, the one drawback with FLIR in the navigation mode is that it has a relatively small field of view and the pilot may lose his visibility at night, or in poor weather, once he looks outside the cockpit (even if the display is projected on to his HUD). The solution to this problem is NVGs. Using image-intensifying (II) tubes mounted on the pilot's flying helmet, NVGs turn available light sources (photons) into electrons, artificially intensifying them and then re-projecting them in the eyepiece. Thus NVGs allow the pilot to see a clearer view beyond the cockpit at night providing, of course, there is some form of existing light to be detected. However, in order to see his head-down instrumentation within the cockpit, suitable panel lighting must be installed.

The first major application of NVGs is for helicopter night operations, and several systems are in service. Ferranti has one set of NVGs in service and under production for the UK MoD, using EEV II tubes, and GEC Avionics has sold its Cat's Eyes system to the US Marine Corps. In the United States, ANVIS (Advanced Night Vision Instrumentation System) NVGs produced by Bell & Howell, Hughes Aircraft, ITT and Litton, among others, are commonplace now. It is in the field of fixed-wing aviation that further development is necessary. The need for NVGs to be externally mounted on the pilot's 'bone dome' (as the flying helmet is usually known to the air crew) can cause problems if he has to eject from his aircraft. These problems are

▼
To improve visibility for pilots flying at night, night vision goggles (NVG) have been developed. This example is the GEC Avionics Cat's Eyes system, which has been sold to the US Marine Corps and was used operationally during the Gulf War. (GEC Avionics)

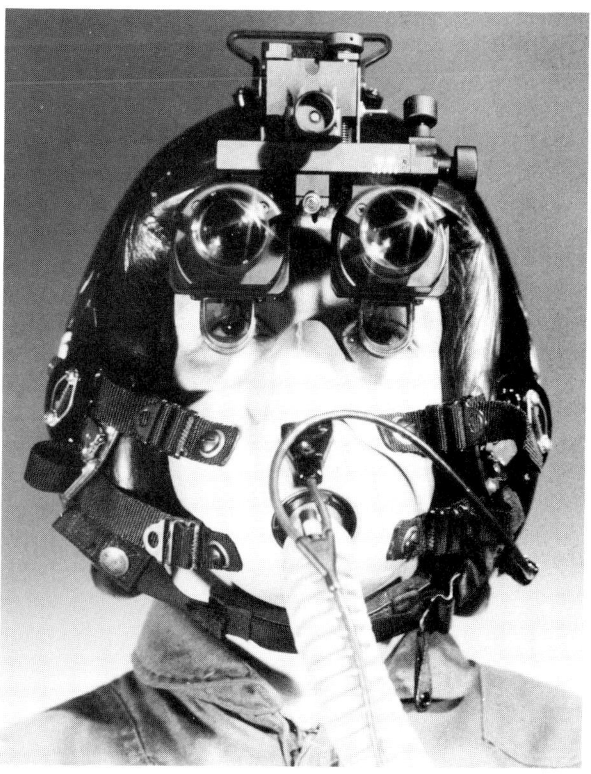

gradually being addressed, and as we move towards the turn of the century they are likely to be solved.

More traditionally, navigation is supplied by an inertial system, using three gyros in a stabilized platform. Hitherto these gyros were mechanical and thus inertial navigation systems (INS) were bulky items to fit into aircraft. However, recent developments have led to the use of laser gyros which are put together in a 'ring' of three systems – hence the term 'ring laser gyro', or RLG. Such RLG inertial navigation systems have cut down considerably on the size of the INS and, at the same time, improved its accuracy.

Usually connected with an INS of any form is a moving map display which pinpoints the aircraft's position. As the aircraft moves along its track, so the map moves as well, always showing the pilot his position. Originally, moving maps were dependent on the map data being held on film and projected on to the display, but other means, including optical discs, are now being introduced, again cutting down on size and, at the same time, increasing the map area available.

Satellite navigation is the latest 'nav aid' in military service. The United States is in the process of launching a series of some 20 Navstar global positioning satellites (GPS) in orbit around the Earth. These transmit signals which can be picked up by GPS receivers on aircraft (and on ships or land vehicles as well), and by using the co-ordinates obtained the position of the aircraft is fixed. There are several modes of signal which can be 'tapped', depending on the type of receiver equipment installed, which for US military use is a five-channel set. The full GPS system has yet to be completed, but sufficient satellites were in orbit in 1991 to allow the systems' operational use during the Gulf War. For the future, most combat aircraft and some guided weapons will have the ability to interrogate the GPS for mid-course updates to pre-programmed target co-ordinates.

The most recent innovation, yet to become operational but now in the final stages of development, is called Terrain-Reference Navigation (TRN). TF/TA radar shows the pilot what is ahead of him and allows him (or the autopilot) to fly above the high ground as he approaches it; alternatively, it can allow him to fly around the high ground, effectively masking the aircraft from ground radar detection. What it cannot provide is information on what sort of terrain lies over the other side of the hill that he is flying over or around. This is where TRN enters the scene.

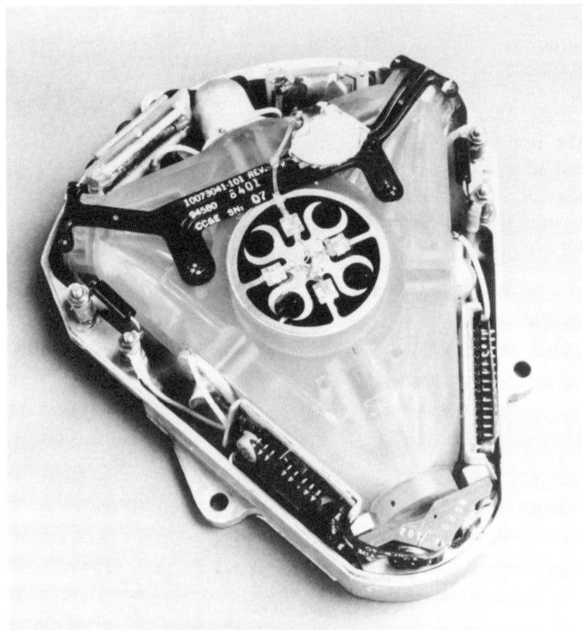

The bulk of the world's land masses are mapped, and the contour lines have been converted into digitized terrain elevation data (DTED). By using this data, stored on board the aircraft, and comparing the information with returns from a radar altimeter, an accurate fix as to exactly where the aircraft is over the ground can be made. Once the aircraft's position is established (using INS or GPS to bring the system into the 'ball park') and the 'fix' obtained, then the area over which it is flying can be presented to the pilot on a map display. This not only shows him his position over the ground but also can be fed into the autopilot to allow a

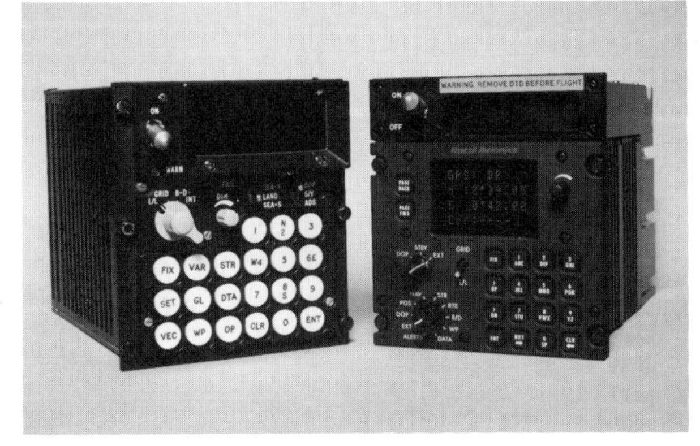

◄ Honeywell of the United States is one of the leading pioneers of ring laser gyro (RLG) development, which has improved the reliability and accuracy and reduced the size of systems requiring gyros for stabilization. Today the company supplies a high proportion of the world's RLGs for navigation, guidance and reference systems for both military and civil aviation. (Honeywell)

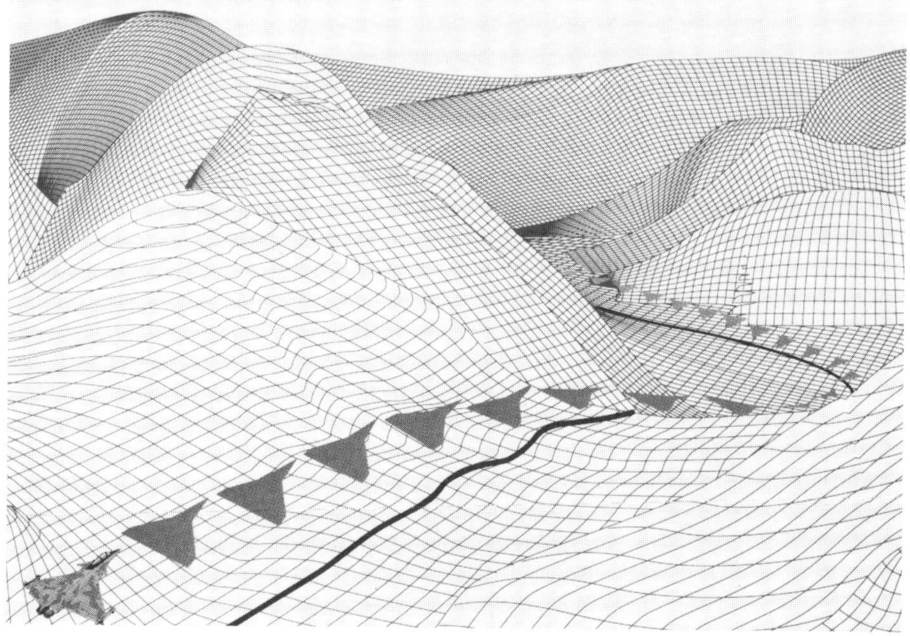

► This diagram illustrates the use of the RBE2 radar in terrain-following/terrain-avoidance (TF/TA) mode. However, the visualization of the terrain itself illustrates the application of digital terrain data as used in terrain profile matching to avoid switching to the active TF/TA mode. (Thomson-CSF)

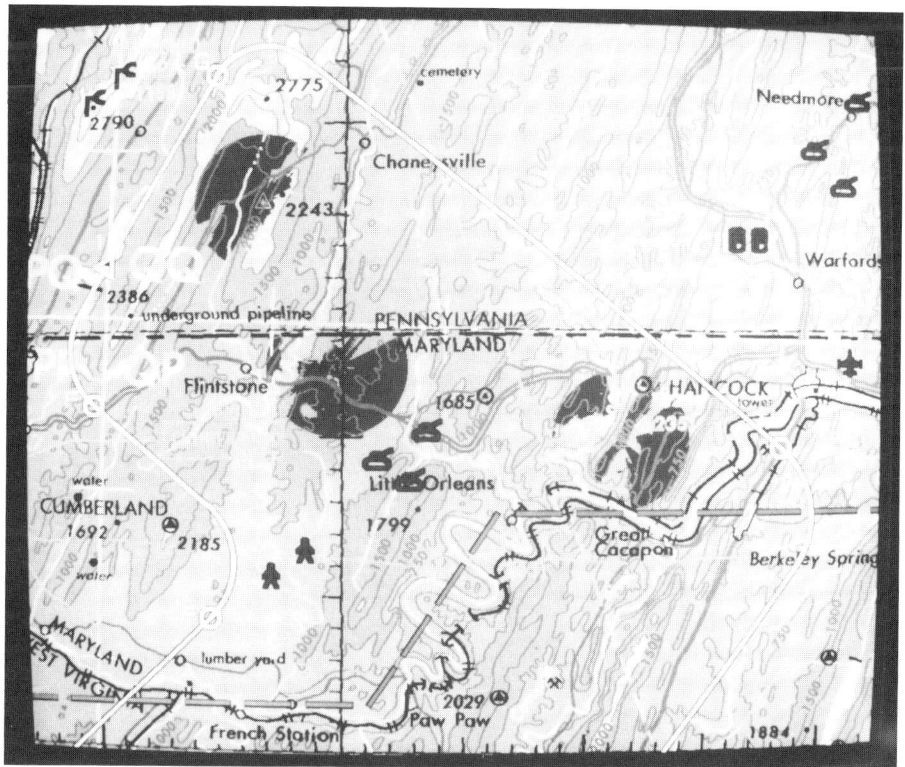

► Replacing first-generation, electro-mechanical, film-based projected map displays in the current Harrier GR.5/7 (and other) combat aircraft is the Digital Colour Map Unit (DCMU). This GEC Avionics DCMU can carry the data to project an area the size of Europe in one avionics box. (GEC Avionics)

◄ The old and the new: to the left, the Racal Avionics Tactical Air Navigation System (TANS) and, to the right, the SuperTANS, which incorporates facilities for receiving GPS/Navstar data. Virtually all UK helicopters used in Operation 'Granby' during the Gulf War were equipped with SuperTANS at short notice. (Racal Avionics)

terrain-avoidance flight path to be flown. It has other uses as well, to which we shall return.

The parallel developments which have allowed TRN to become a reality have been the techniques of data compression into readily accessible and 'intelligent' (i.e. re-programmable in flight) stores, together with high-speed processors to recall the data in real time. In the UK, three companies have been working on such systems: British Aerospace Dynamics with TERPROM, Ferranti with Penetrate and GEC Avionics with Spartan. Across the Atlantic, the Harris Corporation are working on the Digital Terrain Management/Display (DTM/D) system, using the Harris digital map-generation system and a colour multi-function display provided by Bendix; while the Hughes Aircraft Company's Radar Systems Group and TI have developed the Airborne Electronic Terrain Map System (AETMS). AETMS has now been succeeded by the Integrated Terrain Access and Retrieval System (ITARS) and Hughes and Harris are working on competing systems under a

▲▲◄
The pilot's finger points to the display of the E-Systems APR-39 radar warning receiver display in the cockpit of a US combat aircraft. The relatively small space required for the display makes it a basic essential in the electronic defence suite of any modern aircraft. (E-Systems)

▲◄
Once a radar lock-on is detected, aircraft can deploy decoys in an attempt to jam the radar or spoof the missile. This photograph shows the Matra Saphir system launching flares to decoy IR-seeking missiles. (Matra Defence)

▲
As radar-guided missiles become more discriminating, chaff becomes less effective as a decoy. This drawing shows the Texas Instruments GEN-X RF expendable decoy, under development for the US Navy. It emits radar-like signals to lure incoming missiles away from the target aircraft. (Texas Instruments)

▲►
Visible under the starboard wings of these two RAF Tornado GR.1s on patrol during Operation 'Granby' is the NobelTech systems (formerly PEAB) BOZ-series chaff dispenser. The aircraft carry the complementary GEC Sky Shadow ECM jamming pod on the port outer pylons. (Crown Copyright)

USAF Aeronautical Systems Division contract from Wright-Patterson AFB. ITARS displays colour-coded surface features and man-made structures and automatically shares its data with other on-board systems such as INS/GPS, TF/TA radar and FLIR, thus eliminating the need for manual input by the pilot.

Although offering the same basic function, each system sets out to solve the detail in a different way. For example, the system chosen for the RAF's Tornado GR.4 update, Spartan, is the result of work done by GEC Avionics for over ten years. It uses a solid-state storage system (which the company considers to be the most flexible of the storage systems investigated), although other systems, such as the optical disc, can be used. The DTED data can be stored on one card, and other cards can be used for such information as low-flying obstacles, intelligence data, mission data and cultural (i.e. roads, towns, rivers, etc.) data. This storage system is used in GEC's Digital Colour Map Unit for the RAF's Harrier GR.7 update. Spartan's DTED database covers an area in excess of 800,000 sq. km. The company claims a high mean time between failure (MTBF), in excess of 3,000 hours, and all this is contained in one three-quarters ATR short LRU box with a low power consumption of less than 150 watts.

Electronic Warfare

The use of electronic warfare (EW) was dramatically illustrated in the opening phases of Operation 'Desert Storm' in January 1991. It is an all-embracing science, originally known as electronic countermeasures (ECM), which can intrude across radar and passive sensor technology as well as having its own highly specialized features. In simple language, EW is the detection of threats to the aircraft and their identification and neutralization by either passive or active means. Going one step beyond, offensive EW is used for the

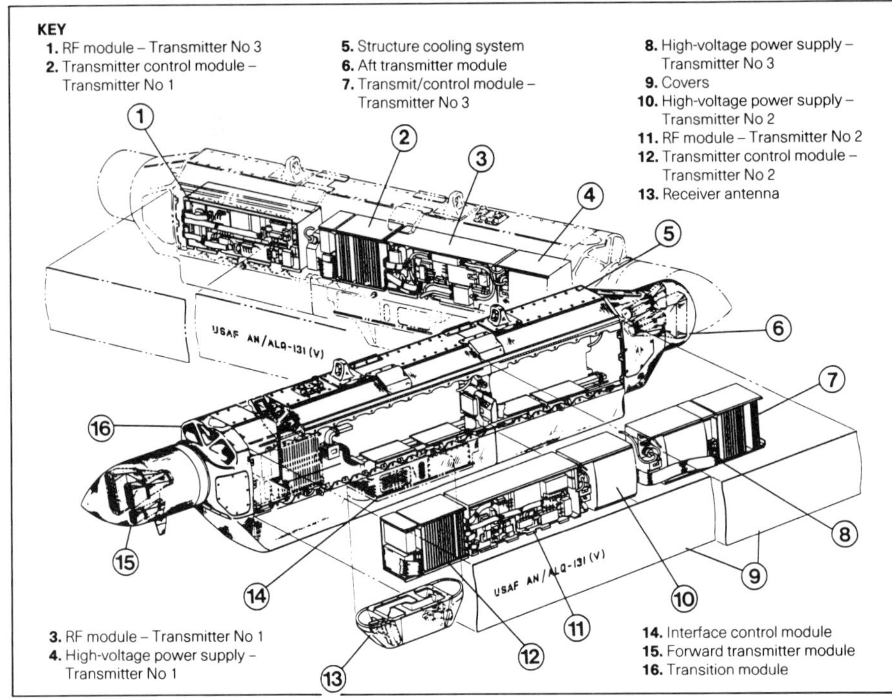

▶ **The only dedicated EW aircraft on the US Navy and Marine Corps inventory is the Grumman EA-6B Prowler. These aircraft were heavily used during the Gulf War, doing sterling service in neutralizing Iraqi radar systems in the van of incoming Coalition air strikes. (Grumman)**

◀ **One of the more widely used ECM jamming pods in US service is the Westinghouse ALQ-131 system. This cutaway drawing shows the component parts of the system. (Westinghouse)**

suppression of enemy defences to create 'safe corridors' along which intruding aircraft can safely penetrate air defence systems to deliver their ordnance, or feints against which enemy air defences are committed. The Brunswick Defense Tactical Air-Launched Decoy (TALD), used by the US Navy and Marine Corps during the Gulf War, is now said to have been what Iraqi sources claimed as the 'hundreds' of coalition aircraft shot down – they actually felled a lot of TALDs.

EW can be as simple or as sophisticated as an air force deems fit for any particular aircraft type, commensurate with its role or mission and the funding available. To illustrate the point, let us build up an aircraft EW suite from the basics through to a fully comprehensive system. The basic threat to any combat aircraft, whether defensive or offensive, is detection by either airborne or ground-based radar. Thus the radar warning receiver (RWR) was born. Alone, this can only indicate to a pilot that he is being 'painted' by a radar beam and, usually, the cockpit display can indicate the quadrant from which the threat emanates. Taken a stage further, the RWR has developed into a missile warning and/or laser warning system as well, taking in more threats. In order to make sensible use of this information, the RWR is usually tied to some form of decoy dispensing system, either chaff or IR flares. The chaff – hair-thickness metallized fibres cut to reflect on particular wavelengths – is to 'spoof' the radar, be it from an intercepting fighter or a missile seeker head, into thinking that there is a bigger target close to hand, on to which the missile is seduced. IR flares do the same job against heat-seeking missiles or sensors. So a basic EW suite would consist of the threat warning system and a decoy dispensing system. Both are easily accommodated on today's and tomorrow's combat aircraft.

The next stage comes with the addition of an active jamming or ECM system. As such equipment was originally developed, it was mounted in a pod, which was then carried on an external weapons pylon. These ECM pods were able to respond with radar-jamming signals on pre-set frequencies most likely to be encountered. Recent developments have made these ECM sets able automatically to adjust frequencies to match detected threats. It was then but one step to include such systems within the airframe design, enabling the external weapons pylon to revert to its original role. The plot thickens and the EW suite expands into

sophistication. Internal jamming systems are now designed into combat aircraft from concept, although some systems can be retrofitted into existing designs.

To avoid long lists of manufacturers and a formidable lexicon of the various EW systems, which may bore all but the dedicated reader, let one case study of defensive EW suffice. During the Falklands conflict in 1982, both RN Sea Harrier FRS.1s and RAF Harrier GR.3s went into action without any form of EW beyond an RWR. Bundles of chaff were carried in the underfuselage airbrake compartment as no decoy dispensers were fitted. For the RAF's follow-on force of Harrier GR.5/7 aircraft, the Marconi Zeus integrated warning and jamming system is installed, linked to a Tracor ALE-40 Tactical Decoy System (TACDS), capable of carrying both chaff and flares. This uses a solid-state microprocessor which accepts input from the threat warning system, air data computer and throttle transducers to determine the optimum deployment of chaff or flares. A recent purchase of NobelTech (formerly PEAB, then Bofors Electronics) BOL chaff dispensers, specifically configured to fit in the LAU-7 launch rails for Sidewinder self-defence air-to-air missiles, allows the ALE-40s to carry a full complement of flares. The final phase of the Harrier GR.5/7 EW suite is the addition (due late in 1991) of the GEC-Plessey Avionics PVS 2000 pulse-Doppler missile approach warner. Once all these ingredients come together, the Harrier GR.5/7 will be one of the best EW-equipped combat aircraft in Europe.

Moving on to offensive EW, there are two areas of interest. One concerns the stand-off and escort jamming aircraft and the other the defence-suppression aircraft, more generally referred to as 'Wild Weasels' after the USAF codename for such aircraft used in the Vietnam War. There are only two current dedicated jamming types and both use, basically, the same system: the US Navy's Grumman EA-6B Prowler and the USAF's EF-111A Raven, the latter a conversion by Grumman of the original model of General Dynamic's F-111 strike aircraft. The common suite used is the Eaton Corporation's ALQ-99 stand-off tactical jamming system, which is claimed to be the first such system with real-time digital processing to determine the nature of threat signals and automatically assign jamming priorities.

The Prowler has received two increased capability (ICAP) improvements since entering service in 1971 and a third ADCAP (advanced capability) modification is in hand. The primary features of this improvement are the installation of the Lockheed/Sanders ALQ-149 communications jammer and the provision to carry two TI AGM-88A Harm (High-speed Anti-Radiation Missiles) to launch against enemy radars, the US Navy having no dedicated Wild Weasels. The Raven has, and continues to receive, equivalent updates, but without the Harm capability as the USAF prefers the dedicated Wild Weasel approach.

The current in-service Wild Weasel is a conversion of the ubiquitous Phantom to F-4G standard. The nose-mounted 20mm gun has been replaced by an APR-38 radar homing and warning system (RHAWS), which is the prime 'emission locator', and the ability to carry the AGM-45 Shrike, AGM-78 Standard ARM and AGM-88A Harm anti-radar missiles. More recently, the USAF has adopted a policy of using a Harm-equipped F-16C operating alongside an F-4G to improve the effectiveness of the Wild Weasel concept. Before the Gulf War, the USAF had decided to withdraw the F-4G from service. Its success in the war has brought about a change of mind and, until a replacement is found (most likely a modified F-16 but possibly a variant of the Tornado ECR model), the F-4G will be retained.

The Tornado ECR (Electronic Combat and Recon-

◄ **This picturesque pose of a Wild Weasel team belies the potency of the system. The darker F-4G Advanced Wild Weasel is equipped with an emitter-location system for finding enemy AAA radars, together with the AGM-88A Harm missile for knocking them out; the accompanying F-16C also carries a pair of Harms to improve the suppression of enemy air defences. (Texas Instruments)**

naissance) version, developed for Germany's Luftwaffe, is the nearest that European air forces have got to a dedicated EW/Wild Weasel aircraft. It is being equipped with an emission locator and provision to launch the Harm missile. Other avionics improvements, including a reconnaissance system, are also being installed.

As can be seen, EW is a complex subject, and the foregoing has but scratched the surface. Again, the driver for most of the technology is the microprocessor and its associated software: the laws of physics cannot change, but the ways in which they can be applied are improving daily.

Communications

Without effective communications – a subject frequently ignored by aviation writers – no tactical or strategic situation can be pursued to advantage. The reader will be well aware of the ease with which he saw reports direct from the Middle East war zone during the build-up and prosecution of the Gulf conflict. The author remembers the ease with which he would telephone the coalition's Joint Press Facility in Riyadh daily during the war, to check on details not covered by the mass media. His contact was a 'poacher turned gamekeeper' – a freelance writer on the author's magazine who was also in the Territorial Army and had volunteered for a tour of duty in the Gulf handling the world's press. Indeed, the situation worked to his advantage as well, as he would shamelessly ring the author in the UK to check on some obscure piece of information to which he had not ready reference, in order to satisfy a press enquiry at his end. This may appear to be a digression but it makes the point.

Airborne communications is as complex a subject as EW and is riddled with as many systems and acronyms. If one accepts that modern combat aircraft need a sensible selection of radio communications as their role requires – usually a mix of HF, UHF and VHF AM/FM equipment – then two criteria for modern 'comms' emerge: the need to maintain secure communications and the need to distribute the information in real time, in order to take the initiative, are paramount. The use of cryptography and transmission techniques such as frequency-hopping are now commonplace. Again, the microprocessor and software are the key to effectiveness. By way of example, during the build-up to the Gulf War, many British, Canadian and French combat aircraft were quickly fitted with US 'Have Quick' secure radios, in order to be compatible with US forces, who had by far the largest number of combat aircraft in the war zone.

For an example of real-time distribution of information, one can do no better than outline the basics of the US joint-service JTIDS (Joint Tactical Information Distribution System) programme. This will provide, when fully implemented, a flexible, multiple-user tactical information exchange service between surface and airborne military units and their commands, using a technique known as Time Division Multiple Access (TDMA). Put simply, each member of a JTIDS network is allocated the time slots to accommodate his input messages into the system, via the TDMA. These inputs would automatically include identification and navigation data in addition to specialized target information such as target acquisition data. All users can continuously monitor and sample the database for such information as they require. The database is broadcast on digital data and voice links, using spread-spectrum, coded and frequency-hopping techniques. Depending on the type of aircraft, a different type of JTIDS terminal is applicable. The initial emphasis was on the land/air use and the Class 1 terminal's prime airborne user is the E-3 Sentry. Class 2 terminals will be for the F-15 and F-16. JTIDS has also been specified for use in the UK's air defence network (on the RAF's Sentry AEW.1 and Tornado F.3) and also on French E-3s.

The Future

If one can bring all the elements of avionics together, one can see science fiction soon becoming science fact. The rapid developments in computer science are the key to virtually every new system and, most importantly, their integration into a whole. Indeed, one could ask whether air crew are now necessary. In some cases they are not, and the use of remotely piloted vehicles (RPVs), increasingly known as unmanned air vehicles (UAVs), in specialized roles like reconnaissance and surveillance, is an indication of this trend. However, whatever the level of sophistication, there is still a need to keep a man 'in the loop'. It will be a very long time before the Mark One Mod One Human Brain can be totally replaced by a computer, however clever its software and however fast its processing speed.

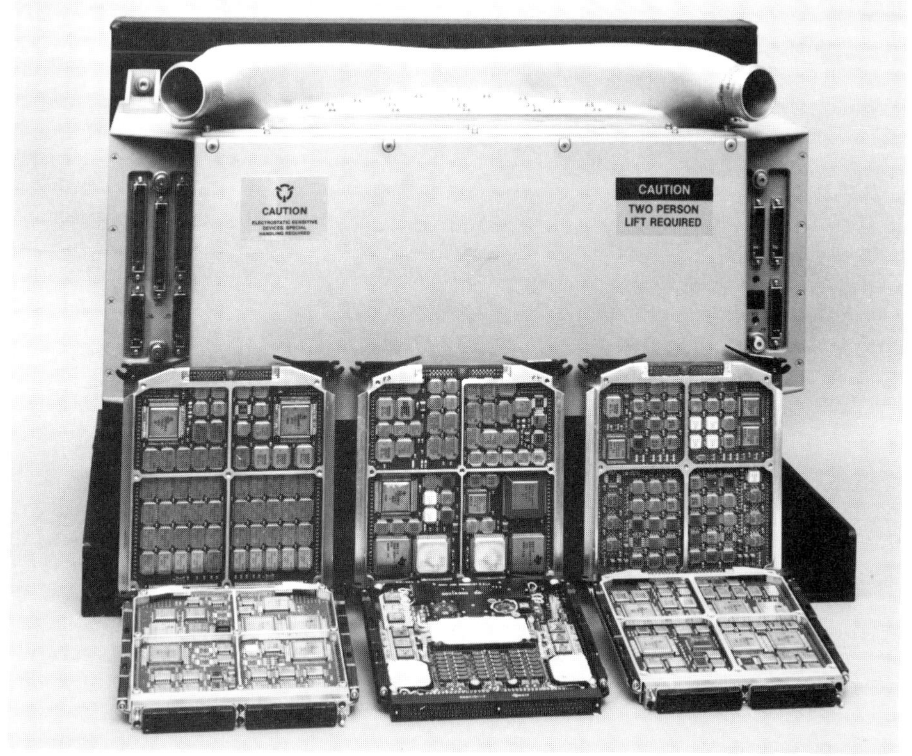

▶ The key to the development of all avionics is the computer system. These, more than any other feature of the systems, are basically 'black boxes' in appearance. This is the mission display processor developed by Texas Instruments for the winning YF-22A ATF contender. It is part of a modular avionics package developed for the ATF programme. The processor's functions are implemented on standard SEM-E format with three-quarter size modules. The module family includes data processor, memory, power supply, timing and control, multipurpose interface and 1553 databus modules. (Texas Instruments)

The reason for every combat aircraft ever built is simple – to prosecute war. Even unarmed combat aircraft (if that is not a contradiction in terms) have a role – to support the fighting machines. War means weapons, and, without them, everything that has gone before is irrelevant.

Guns

Pioneer air fighter Captain Louis Strange RFC wrote in his memoires of the First World War, *Recollections of an Airman*, that '... every man who goes into the air in a fighting machine is a gun layer – first and last ...' Over 70 years later, speaking with an RAF Tornado F.3 pilot in 1988, the author was told, 'The gun seems obsolete but you never know when you may get into a situation ... [where you can] kill with a gun better than anything else. I'd never want them to take it away.' Both statements contain a basic element of truth which has stood the test of time.

The use of guns on modern combat aircraft now comes third in the priority of air-to-air weaponry, after medium-range and short-range air-to-air missiles (MRAAMs and SRAAMs, respectively) – witness the code-phrase 'Fox Three' for gunfire kills in current air crew parlance. However, as the USAF found during the mid-1960s over the skies of Vietnam, the gun still has its place. If one discounts the use of the gun as a defensive armament on the few remaining 'traditional' bombers in service – the Soviet Tu-16 'Badger' and the Tu-95/142 'Bear', their Chinese 'copies' and the USAF's ageing B-52G/H models – then the use of the gun is now confined to air defence and ground attack aircraft, plus dedicated attack or anti-armour helicopters. Other aircraft types, notably trainers (of all descriptions), transport helicopters and some maritime patrol or surveillance aircraft, are equipped to carry guns or gun pods for specific tasks.

The gun represents a flexible weapon system in many peacetime scenarios. To adapt the nautical concept of a 'shot across the bows', one is tempted to wonder whether a few rounds of 23mm cannon fire across the nose of KAL Flight 007 would have concentrated the airliner crew's mind on Russian concern over its flight-path. As history sadly records, the Soviets had intercepted the Boeing 747 with Su-15 'Flagons' and their only resort was to release an air-to-air missile. Once launched, the result was terminal. Similarly, a small cargo boat engaged in nefarious operations in some far-flung archipelago might be unconcerned at a patrolling aircraft overhead. If the aircraft is equipped with a gun pod, then shots can be, literally, placed across the ship's bows (or anywhere else, should the need arise).

Automatic weapons used on aircraft have followed the traditional weapons terminology: calibres up to 15mm are machine guns and fire bullets, cannon range from 20mm up to 35mm and fire explosive shells. The rule is, simply, the greater the calibre, the greater the range and weight of projectile. A 7.62mm machine gun (in the air-to-ground role) can throw a 10g bullet to an effective range of 500m and a 12.7mm weapon throws a 45g bullet to around 1,000m. Moving upwards to 20mm, ranges of 1,700m are the order, with a projectile weighing between 125 and 144g, while a 25mm cannon can effectively reach some 2,200m with a 500g projectile.

The refinement of guided weapons, particularly air-to-air missiles, led to the fallacy in the mid-1950s through to the mid-1960s that a gun armament, particularly for air defence operations, was no longer required. In the United States, the F-102 and F-106 interceptors were produced without a gun armament, as were the F-4B/C/D models of the Phantom; while in the UK, the two 20mm cannon were deleted from the armament of the Lightning on the F.3 and early F.6 models. In the Soviet Union, both the Sukhoi Su-15/21

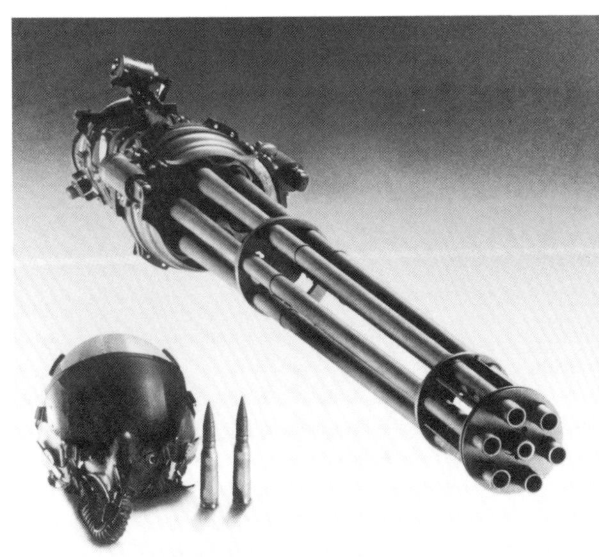

'Flagon' and Tupolev Tu-28P 'Fiddler' were purely missile-armed fighters. Experience, particularly over Vietnam, showed the need for the flexibility a gun provides, and the GE 20mm M61A1 Vulcan gun was retrofitted to the F-106 while a new version of the Phantom, the F-4E, had to be developed to take a nose-mounted M61A1 Vulcan. Since then, the M61A1 has armed the current range of USAF and US Navy fighters. Twin 30mm Aden cannon were later retrofitted to the Lightning F.6, while the RAF's Tornado F.3s are armed with a single 27mm Mauser cannon. The Soviet Union's MiG-23 'Flogger' has a 23mm gun while the MiG-29 'Fulcrum' and Sukhoi Su-27 'Flanker' both have 30mm cannon as standard fit.

Such weapons can be tied into the parent aircraft's fire control system, with appropriate symbology projected on to the pilot's HUD, or used in the more traditional way, via boresighting techniques. The high rates of fire from modern weapons mean that half-second bursts are usually sufficient to damage any aircraft unfortunate enough to take hits. According to an RAF Tornado F.3 pilot, in modern air defence operations, if the gun is used, 'it only needs a couple of [bullets to hit] ... a fighter-sized target and he's going to be badly placed ... [providing] you establish a line [of bullets] and put a decent number of bullets in the air ...' It is snap-shooting in the air. Longer bursts of fire, as depicted in Hollywood movies, are totally unrealistic, as the ammunition capacity of the fighter would be exhausted in no time. Air combat techniques of the First and Second World Wars, even of the Korean War, whereby the attacker follows his target to put himself into a killing situation, are 'out of the window' in the modern environment. 'Turning and burning' is no longer the name of the game: killing with MRAAMs beyond visual range is preferable – and safer for the fighter air crew. Yet, as the Tornado F.3 pilot told the author, 'I'd never want them to take it away.'

Where the prime role of a combat aircraft is ground attack, the availability of gun armament is just as desirable. Although many ground attack or strike aircraft tend to carry SRAAMs for self-defence, having a gun as well is a great morale booster for, even when the missiles are gone, the pilot can still shoot back. As an air-to-ground weapon in a sophisticated Central Front scenario, the gun is no longer a prime system, despite the advances in ammunition development. It is seen rather as a weapon for use on targets of opportunity, particularly after the main armament of bombs or air-to-surface missiles has been expended. Even the formidable 30mm GAU-8/A of the A-10A Thunderbolt is no longer considered a prime weapon – the aircraft pylons carry a large number of Maverick missiles. The reason for this is simple: when going for a gun strafe, the aircraft is far more exposed to ground fire, particularly by shoulder-launched SAMs.

However, in lower-intensity military environments, particularly when an aircraft is operating against a

◀ **The latest version of the GE 20mm M61A1 Vulcan gun offers lighter weight, improved reliability and maintainability and the ability to fire M50-series and the new MP ammunition, in addition to being compatible with existing systems. (General Electric)**

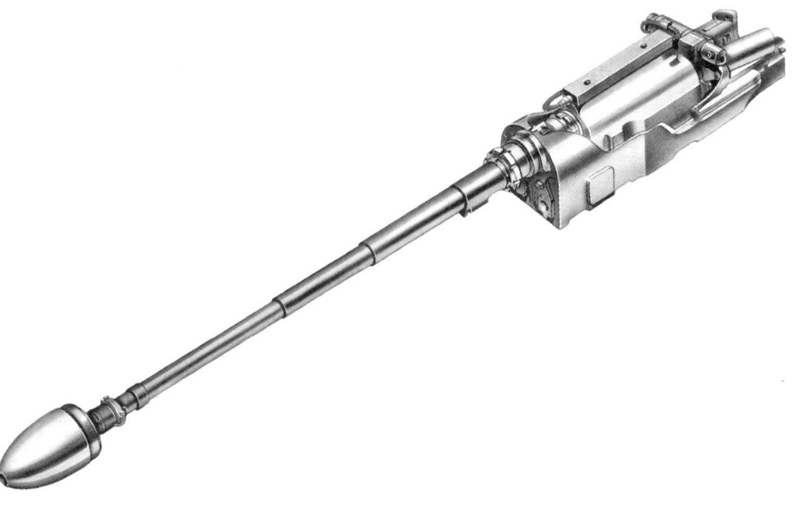

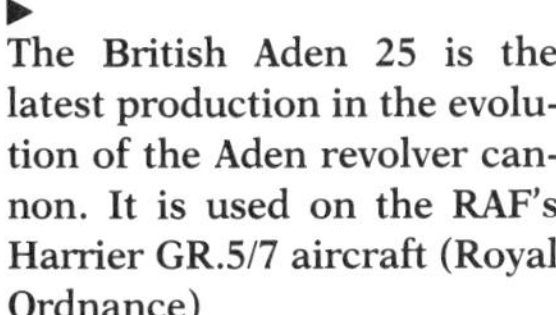

▶ **The British Aden 25 is the latest production in the evolution of the Aden revolver cannon. It is used on the RAF's Harrier GR.5/7 aircraft (Royal Ordnance)**

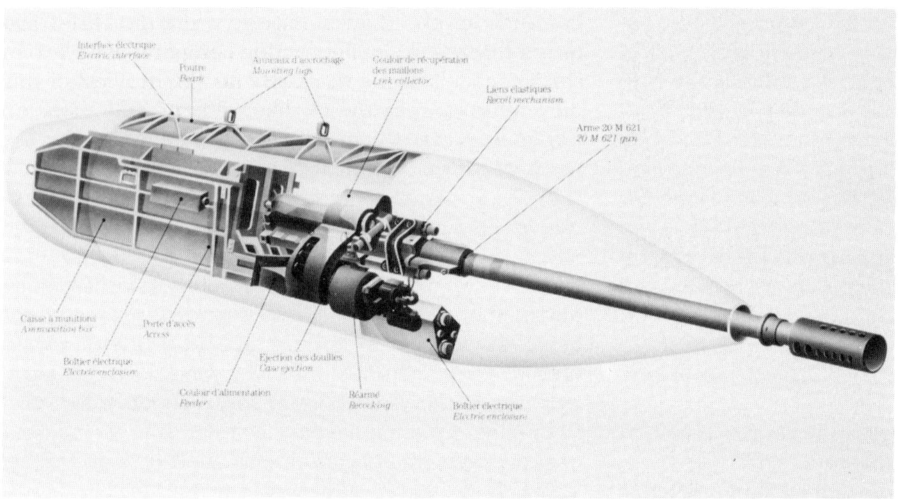

◄
The anatomy of a gun pod – in this case the French M621 20mm pod produced by GIAT Industries.

►
As an example of helicopter armament, this external mounting assembly, developed by Fabrique National of Belgium, shows the company's light external pintle mount with a 7.62mm general-purpose machine gun, together with a 12.7mm (0.5in) heavy machine gun pod.

less sophisticated enemy, the exposure to ground fire is less and, so, opportunities exist for air-to-ground gunfire attacks. It is here that the gun pods carried by trainer aircraft or utility helicopters, pressed into the light strike or ground attack roles, come into their own. The results of operations using these systems are rarely as lethal as the attackers might wish, but as they are usually conducted as part of an air/ground operation they will be sufficient to keep the defenders' heads down. At this level, too, come the crew-served weapons deployed on such utility helicopters, carried either on an internal carriage/seat mount or semi-externally on a pintle-mount. They are as much for crew morale as for effective air-to-ground use but, in experienced hands, can be efficacious.

The development of the helicopter gunship, followed by the dedicated attack helicopter, has proved the most useful catalyst in airborne gun development in recent years. Again, the guns were initially considered to be 'area weapons', for keeping heads down during an assault operation. By combining a turreted gun, which can be aimed by the air crew, with anti-armour missile systems or rocket pods, operators found that they could use the gun more accurately and to greater effect. Such was the threat posed by Western anti-armour helicopter forces that Soviet designers refined their Mi-24 'Hind' series so that they could combat NATO helicopters. They have developed their own 'Apache-lookalike', the Mi-28 'Havoc', and gone for the world's first 'anti-helicopter helicopter', the Kamov 'Hokum'. The response to these Soviet threats has been rapid development of helicopter-borne AAMs such as the FIM-92 Stinger and the addition of forward-firing gun installations or underslung turrets on helicopters previously unarmed in any form.

The availability of gun pods has also been an added advantage for manufacturers of utility/patrol aircraft with underwing hardpoints. These gun pods can also be carried and offer an easy option of adding the flexibility of gun systems to what is, essentially, an unarmed aircraft. A suggested scenario has already been described.

The weapons themselves can be classified by the type of action they employ in their operation. The simple reciprocating or linear action can be used by both machine gun and cannon. The gun can be operated by recoil of the fired cartridge, by its gas propellant or by a combination of both. The rate of fire is dictated by the amount of time taken to extract the cartridge and replace it with a new round. For air-to-air use, a high rate of fire is required, in order to achieve sufficient 'punch' on the target, while for a helicopter-mounted weapon with an air-to-ground function a lower rate of fire is acceptable. The problem with such self-powered weapons, operated by propellent gas pressure, is that a single misfire can stop the gun.

By using an externally powered weapon, the misfired round will be extracted and the gun will continue to fire. The McDonnell Douglas Helicopter Company (MDHC) has developed a family of weapons known as 'Chain Guns' which combine the compactness of linear action weapons with the reliability inherent in

externally powered guns. Here the bolt's reciprocating movement is powered by a self-contained chain drive running over four sprocket-wheels, one of which is powered by an electric motor. The size of the chain's 'racetrack' is dictated by the time required to hold the breech closed for as long as is necessary to allow the burnt gases to escape. Three main variants have been developed, in 7.62mm, 25mm and 30mm calibres. The first and last have airborne applications, the latter in the AH-64 Apache attack helicopter, while the 25mm version is used on US ground infantry fighting vehicles. They will continue to be used for many years to come.

Demands for increased rates of fire (cyclic rates) led to the development of the revolver cannon in Germany by Mauser, during the Second World War. The ammunition is fed into a five-chambered rotating cylinder, driven by the reciprocating action of a gas-operated slide. This breaks down the operating cycle into a series of stages, reducing the time taken between shots, thereby increasing the rate of fire. The MG213C/20 was able to fire at a cyclic rate of 1,500rds/min compared with the 1,100rds/min of the single-chamber, linear-action MG213A. A number of weapons were developed along this principle in the postwar period – the French 30mm DEFA 553, the British 30mm Aden and the US M39 – while the latest in the Mauser range is the BK27 developed for Tornado and other aircraft. Improvements to this concept have been made with the electrical or mechanical controls and in the ammunition developed for use by the weapons. Thus, the Aden 25 uses the revolver principle but with improved ammunition, while the DEFA 554 uses a three-stage loading action compared with two in earlier models of the range. By far the heaviest of this particular genre is the Oerlikon 30mm KCA, used on the JA.37 Viggen, which weighs some 300lb. It can, however, fire a 1.96lb cartridge at 1,030m/sec.

Another way of increasing the rate of fire is to use two barrels in parallel, the recoil of one activating the other. The first significant development in this principle was the Gast Gun, developed by Germany during the First World War but never put into operational service. It was not until the mid-1950s that the principle was 'rediscovered' by Hughes Helicopters and used on its 20mm Mk. 11 cannon. Using both recoil force and gas pressure, two belts of ammunition fed into an eight-chambered cylinder. This was able to insert two cartridges, fire two and eject two simultaneously, achieving a cyclic rate of 4,200rds/min. It was most widely used in the Mk. 4 gun pod during the mid-1960s. The Soviet Union has been the most enthusiastic user of this type of weapon, in the form of the 23mm GsH-23 on the MiG-21 'Fishbed' series of fighters and later aircraft. It is mounted on the belly of the aircraft and is fed from a magazine located in the fuselage above.

In the United States, Ford Aerospace has developed a 30mm twin-barrel weapon under the Compact High-performance Aerial Gun (CHAG) programme for possible use by the US Advanced Tactical Fighter (ATF). However, during an interview with the author in September 1987, Colonel James A. Fain Jr, Director of the USAF's ATF programme, was categoric in his assertion that both the YF-22A and YF-23A development aircraft would be armed with a version of the venerable M61, the M61A2. In the event, although the M61A2 is to be used, it is being re-engineered and supplied with a new range of ammunition.

This brings us neatly on to the postwar resurrection of the 1861 Gatling principle by General Electric in the United States. Although the revolver concept offered higher rates of fire, the USAF opted, in 1946, to investigate the potential of a modern Gatling gun under the codename 'Project Vulcan'. Using electric power in place of the original hand-crank, a cluster of radial barrels (usually six, although smaller numbers have since been used) rotate around a common axis. Each barrel has its own bolt to feed, fire and extract the ammunition. The bolt is activated by a 'follower' that rides in a cam-track on the fixed housing of the gun.

The result was the M61A1 Vulcan cannon, which typically fires at a rate of 6,000rds/min and can go up go 7,200. It became the standard internal gun armament of USAF fighters, beginning with the F-104 Starfighter and F-105 Thunderchief in 1958. The Vulcan is standard on the F-14 Tomcat, F-15 Eagle, F-16 Fighting Falcon and F/A-18 Hornet and has been adopted by several other nations in their fighter developments – notably by the Italians on their version of the AMX strike fighter.

After the Vulcan, perhaps the most important Gatling development from GE was the 30mm GAU-8/A Avenger, developed for internal mounting in the close air support A-10A Thunderbolt II. A seven-barrel weapon, it has (by Vulcan standards) a relatively modest rate of fire of 2,100 or 4,200rds/min. Designed for ground attack, this weapon fires a new family of lightweight ammunition, using aluminium cases. The API (armour-piercing, incendiary) round is equipped with a depleted uranium core and has been demonstrated as an effective 'tank-killer'. The 430g projectile, with a muzzle velocity of 980m/sec, arrives at its target at 1,200m distance with fourteen times the kinetic energy of the standard US 20mm API round. The Avenger has since been developed into a four-barrel version, the GAU-13/A, which is mounted in a gun pod and offers a similar capability for aircraft such as the F-4, F-5 and A-7. A 25mm version, the GAU-12/U Equalizer, with three barrels, was developed for use on the USMC's AV-8B Harrier II: the system is mounted in belly pods, the port pod housing the gun and the starboard 300 rounds of ammunition, fed across through a faired chute. The Gatling principle has also been applied to the smaller calibres, the GAU-2B/A Minigun in 7.62mm and the GECAL-50 in 12.7mm, for both fixed- and rotary-winged applications. For the future, GE is working on the Cased Telescoped Gun, which uses a round of ammunition with the bullet 'telescoped' into the cartridge case. This allows the bullet to be fired at a given energy for a smaller charge, or vice versa. Details of this USAF project remain highly classified.

Over the years, the 20mm cannon has become recognized as the ideal air-to-air weapon, having a high rate of fire which balances the disadvantage of the relatively low 'punch' the projectile carries. The 30mm calibre weapon has been more suited for ground attack, as a result of the greater lethality of its projectile, which has compensated for its slightly slower rate of fire. This latter characteristic also means a greater exposure for the aircraft, owing to the need to track the target for longer to ensure hits. Apart from application, gun/system weight has also played an important part in the equation, with smaller calibres being adopted in the search for weight-reduction. Recent developments have seen a compromise emerge between these two classic calibres, especially as the trend in fast combat aircraft design has moved towards multi-role capability. Thus 25mm weapons have emerged for the AV-8B/Harrier GR.5 and a 27mm cannon for the Tornado, which has also been adopted for German Alpha Jets and the Swedish JAS.39 Gripen.

The reduction in calibres has been compensated for by improved ammunition design in recent years. In 25mm, the family of ammunition developed for the Bushmaster gun is acknowledged as being particularly potent. In the same calibre, Oerlikon ammunition is highly rated and recent developments include both frangible and fin-stabilized rounds. The 27mm range of ammunition for the BK27 features ballistically matched projectiles of various types fitted with a fuze system, enabling the rounds to operate effectively at high angles of impact. A major innovation in cannon ammunition in recent years has been the Raufoss Multi-Purpose (MP) design, utilizing pyrotechnic initiation to dispense with expensive mechanical fuzing (leaving more space for 'warhead' filling), which gives a considerable enhancement in terminal effects against a wide variety of targets. Already MP ammunition is gaining more acceptance and has been adopted by the US Navy, as well as by the RAF for their Harrier GR.5/7s.

The development of guns for airborne applications is still an important part of aircraft weapons systems. The gun is still highly valued by the air crews themselves and, so, it will continue to be developed. General Electric is pursuing a twin-barrel weapon, the 25mm GE 225, for both air-to-air and air-to-ground applications, while France has developed a new gun, the GIAT 30mm Type 791B, for the Rafale. The European Fighter Aircraft will use a varient of the BK27 weapon used on Tornado. When the F-15 was being developed in the early 1970s, Philco-Ford (now Loral Aeronutronics) developed the 25mm GAU-7/A, using caseless ammunition. As a result of storage problems and uneven propellant burning, this project was dropped in favour of the M61A1. Whether the intervening years have solved these problems is unclear, bearing in mind the fact that caseless ammunition has still to achieve operational status in the infantry weapon field. Other solutions, including the use of liquid propellants, are still some distance away, as is the electro-magnetic 'rail gun', which uses electro-magnetic energy to propel a bullet down the barrel. Whether this type of gun can be successfully shielded from the aircraft's electronic systems, to avoid interference, is a question still to be resolved. However, one thing is certain: whether it is used as a primary weapon, a weapon of opportunity or a weapon of last resort, the gun offers much-needed tactical flexibility.

Air-to-Air Missiles

Fighter aircraft today, whether they be pure interceptors, air superiority aircraft or strike fighters, would be no more effective than their predecessors of 40 years ago were it not for their principal weapons system – the air-to-air missile (AAM), also known as air interception missiles (AIM). Until the early 1980s it would be fair to state that virtually all the AAMs in service around the world were developments of systems which began life in the 1950s and early 1960s. However, the advances in sensors, micro-circuitry, processor miniaturization and rocket propulsion have now resulted in a new generation of missiles, as well as in greatly improved variants of many older designs. Add to these the increased 'operational' experience in the use of such weapons, and the kill probabilities of AAMs today have improved tremendously.

The kill rate of 9 per cent achieved by the AIM-7E Sparrow used by the USAF and US Navy in 1965–68 at the height of the Vietnam War was an important catalyst in the development of the AAM. A more recent US DoD study has shown that, between 1975 and 1985, some 90 per cent of tactical aircraft lost in conflicts worldwide were destroyed by IR-guided missiles – a mixture of AAMs and ground-based, man-portable air defence systems (MANPADS). Every measure has its countermeasure, so, as we have noted, self-defence IR-jammers and chaff/flare dispensers have joined the avionics/EW suites of tactical aircraft and helicopters. To cope with the growing numbers of such countermeasures, missiles – whether heat-seeking or radar-guided – require improved ECCM (electronic counter-countermeasures) and decoy resistance.

For heat-seeking missiles, we are now seeing a move towards imaging infra-red (IIR) seekers, originally developed for air-to-ground missiles such as the Maverick. These are, essentially, small IR-TV cameras which build up a thermal picture of the target aircraft and, through the use of miniature processors on the missile, enable the latter to be directed to the 'softest' part of the fuselage. Low-density platinum silicide arrays, less expensive than the higher-definition sensors on Maverick-type weapons, are being developed. Also in the development stage are 'staring' arrays.

The radar-guided AAMs using semi-active radar (SAR – not to be confused with search-and-rescue or synthetic aperture radar) guidance, developed during the early 1970s, were susceptible to ECM, mainly

▶ This line-up of F-14 Tomcats on board USS *Saratoga* during the Gulf War shows the ubiquitous AIM-9 Sidewinder mounted on the side of the wing pylon carrying an AIM-7 Sparrow. Below this can be seen the nose of an AIM-54 Phoenix BVR missile. (US Navy)

because of their conical scanning mode. Many missiles required the launch aircraft's fire control radar system to remain locked on to the target up to impact. This inherent weakness has now been overcome by the use of monopulse techniques in the seeker. During the 1980s the radar-guided missile took a further step forward with the development and introduction of active radar seekers. Component miniaturization has been the key to this progression, which also allows low-cost interial guidance systems to be installed. Thus missiles are directed by the inertial system sufficiently close to the target to allow the active seeker to lock on and direct the missile to impact. The medium-range (10–100km or beyond visual range, BVR) missile now has access to a 'fire-and-forget' capability. For longer-range work (i.e. beyond 100km) it is possible to allow command updates from the launch aircraft's fire control system to re-direct the missile towards the target, via a one-way data link. While this is not truly a 'fire-and-forget' facility, the distances at which the command signal requires to be transmitted are such that, once updated, the missile becomes autonomous and more accurate.

A target aircraft which uses active jamming in an attempt to spoof the active missile might then fall foul of a further technological 'tweak'. By using techniques developed for air-to-ground, anti-radar missiles (ARMs), a Home-On-Jam (HOJ) mode can also be incorporated within the active seeker. Thus the target may become 'self-illuminating' without realizing it. Incorporating active radar, inertial guidance with command update facilities and HOJ on the latest AAMs makes for a highly sophisticated system. One can quickly see the reasons why the development time of modern AAMs, and their costs, are rising – and why fewer such projects are being initiated.

Looking to the future, the use of fibre-optic guidance, with the AAM trailing a fine optical wire, offers a high band-width and an unjammable communications link. While the US Army is looking at such guidance systems for both anti-tank and anti-aircraft use, the USN, with its Skyray programme, is also investigating optical guidance for AAMs.

Before we turn to current systems, there are two other areas of AAM technology which deserve mention: propulsion and launch systems. Early solid rocket motors emitted significant levels of smoke and flame. These could, under the right circumstances, provide visual clues that indicated the launch of an AAM and affect any IR-based command-to-line-of-sight (CLOS) tracking systems. It has also been shown that these flames could in particular affect the launch aircraft's passive IR sensors. Exhaust plumes from rocket motors have also been known to attenuate radar signals. By the careful addition of suitable chemical compounds to the solid propellant, flame, flash and radar attenuation can be drastically reduced. Such chemicals must also be neutral (or have little effect) in respect of smoke output and should not degrade power. Commercial confidentiality has meant that the exact nature of the compounds used has been little publicized.

Another innovation, being adopted by the General Dynamics/Westinghouse team in their Advanced AAM (AAAM) bid (see below), is a multi-burn solid propellant rocket motor. The design uses a tandem-mounted boost motor and a dual-burn sustainer fitted with jet-tab thrust-vectoring. For engaging high-altitude targets, the sustainer can be re-ignited during the latter stages of flight. Beyond the solid rocket motor, investigations are being carried out into the feasibility of using liquid propellant rockets and, also, air-breathing engines. Work on the former is in a very early stage, while applications for the latter are presently centred on long-range SAMs and air-launched anti-ship missiles. However, Sweden is contemplating a Volvo-developed ramjet for its projected Rb.73 AAM, using a modified Sky Flash airframe; and the Hughes/Raytheon AAAM bid features an integral rocket/ramjet motor, using a solid propellant for the boost phase and switching to the ramjet for a sustainer motor.

For missile carriage and launch, manufacturers usually design their own systems, which tend to be unique to missile type or even sub-variants of a family. For example, there are some ten different launchers required for the plethora of Sidewinder models. The dedication of the missile/launcher situation does not improve interoperability within air arms, to say nothing of that within alliances. Additionally, interface problems can exist between one missile type and its use on a variety of different aircraft. At best, role change times go up and, at worst, an aircraft landing away from a base equipped to operate that type may be unable to be re-armed.

This aspect of missile technology tends to be considered almost as an afterthought in a missile procurement programme and, for the customer, can prove

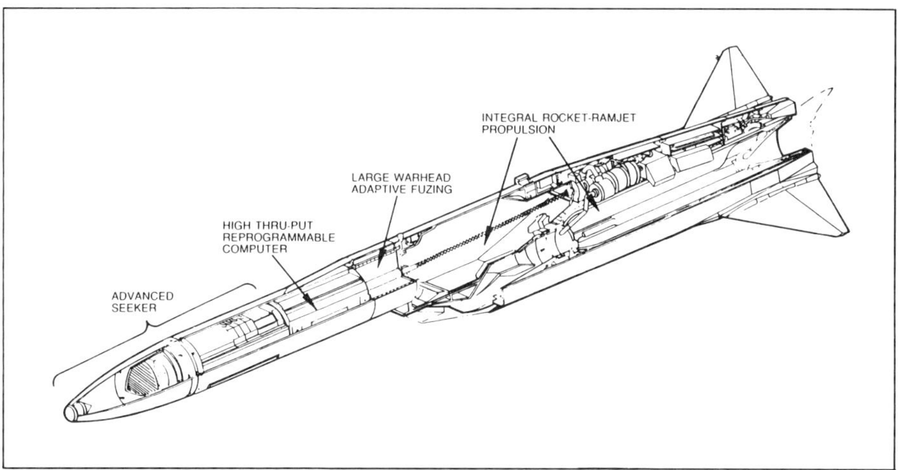

▶ One of the contenders for the US Advanced Air-to-Air Missile programme is this joint venture from Hughes and Raytheon. It uses rocket/ramjet propulsion for long range, while high-capacity on-board processing of data from a high-power active seeker and a passive image sensor offers accurate autonomy. (Hughes)

more costly than anticipated. In an effort to overcome these problems, Frazer-Nash Defence Systems of the UK (now part of Airscrew Howden) has developed what it considers to be a viable solution to this particular problem in the form of a Common Rail Launcher (CRL). Modularity is the key to the CRL, enabling the basic system to be configured to accept a variety of AAMs (and some air-to-ground missiles) by a simple exchange of modules. Indeed, in one configuration, it is possible to accept AIM-9 Sidewinder, AIM-120 AMRAAM and AIM-132 ASRAAM (if this particular project survives) without any modification. The CRL can also accept the Swedish BOL chaff-dispensing system in its rear body, thus saving a weapons pylon.

Having looked at the future, it is also worth looking at the status of some of the major AAM programmes around the world. These systems will be with us through the turn of the century and, as such, indicate the state-of-the-art. Short-range, lightweight AAMs have been developed from MANPADS missiles for use on helicopters, to counter the threat of air combat over the battle area. Leading the field has been the General Dynamics FIM-92 in a version known as Air-to-Air Stinger (ATAS), now re-designated AIM-92. This version entered full-scale development (FSD) in 1984 and US Army service in 1988. In French service, the Matra Mistral (developed from the SATCP family) will arm Gazelle and Tiger helicopters, being aimed by either a helmet- or a roof-mounted ATGW sight. Carriage trials have also been carried out on the US AH-64A Apache helicopter. The Shorts Starstreak system, the MANPADS version of which is now in the FSD phase, has been offered for air-to-air use as Helistreak. A hyper-velocity missile (HMV), capable of attaining Mach 4, the Starstreak/Helistreak has a unique warhead in the form of three kinetic-energy darts, each with a small HE warhead. If development for airborne use proceeds, Helistreak could be in service by about 1994. Meanwhile, a development of Starstreak's predecessor, Javelin, has been equipped with laser-guidance, under the name Starburst. Used in its MANPADS role in the Gulf, this, too, could be adapted for helicopter use.

While most of the missiles in this category are MANPADS-derived, Rockwell International is developing an air-to-air version of its AGM-114 Hellfire antitank missile, under a US Army contract. It involves the evaluation of the Hellfire's inherent capability against airborne targets. The study will include live firing tests and will establish Hellfire's baseline air-to-air performance, providing data for future systems.

Within the Soviet Union, the SA-7 'Grail' MANPADS was first seen in an air-to-air role in the late 1970s. An improved version, SA-7b or 'Strela-2M' as the Soviets know it, was followed by the 'Strela-3' in the mid-1970s. The SA-14 'Gremlin', which is replacing 'Grail', has a more sensitive IR seeker, with IRCM provisions. Although there are no confirmed airborne applications, it is logical to project that 'Gremlins' will be used as AAMs. The same can be said of the latest Soviet MANPADs, the SA-16. Understood to have an all-aspect IR seeker, the SA-16 has a more powerful warhead than the SA-14 and a larger motor, offering greater speeds and longer range.

The classic short-range 'dogfight' AAM must surely be the AIM-9 Sidewinder series. Developed by the US Naval Weapons Center and first flown in 1953, this missile has been widely used by all branches of the US military and has also been widely exported. These and similar missiles are used as primary air-to-air weapons on lightweight fighter interceptors, such as the F-5 series; as secondary weapons on larger, dedicated air defence aircraft, such as the F-14, F-15 and Tornado F.3; and as self-defence weapons for strike/attack aircraft (F-111, Jaguar, etc.) or helicopters (AH-1 Cobra series and AH-64 Apache).

To describe the variety of Sidewinder variants and their use would take a chapter on its own. For our purposes, we shall move forward from the third-generation AIM-9L, which is capable of seeking its target from 'all aspects'. US production began in 1976 and licence-production in Europe and Japan from the early 1980s. The 'Lima' gave a good account of itself with the Fleet Air Arm during the Falklands campaign of 1982, being officially credited with 24 kills out of 27 launches. The AIM-9M, featuring improved IRCM against decoy flares, entered production in the United States in 1982, with a reduced-signature rocket motor. The AIM-9R version, improving on the 'Mike', is now being delivered to the US Navy. The two major US contractors for Sidewinders are Loral Aeronutronics and Raytheon, while Motorola has adapted early-model AIM-9Cs to take an ARM seeker, the converted missiles being re-designated AGM-122A Sidearm. Both Raytheon and Loral are working on technologies for the future Sidewinder, currently known as AIM-9XX.

In Europe, BGT of Germany leads the Euro-Sidewinder production group and has developed an update kit to bring AIM-9J/N/P export models to the 'Lima' standard. Israel's Shafrir 2 and Brazil's MAA-1 are understood to be based on the AIM-9, while the Rafael Python is a development of Shafrir. A 'Chinese copy' of the Sidewinder, designated PL-5, has been produced (not unnaturally) in the PRC, while the Soviet equivalent, the K-13 (NATO designation AA-2 'Atoll') was originally based on an early-model AIM-9B. Further Soviet improvements have been made since the early 1960s, including the development of an SAR-guided version. CATIC of the PRC has produced a version of 'Atoll' designated PL-2.

There are three other short-range dogfight AAMs within the Soviet inventory: the AA-8 'Aphid', a version of the AA-10 'Alamo', and the latest missile, the AA-11 'Archer'. The 'Aphid' (Soviet designation K-60) was

◀ **The Rafale-A development aircraft displays two major air-to-air missiles from Matra Defence of France. On the wing-tips are a pair of R550 Magic 2s, while under the fuselage are four MICA missiles. (Dassault Aviation)**

developed as a tail-chase missile in the late 1960s and has been improved to have all-aspect capability. The IR-guided version of 'Alamo' offers longer range over the 'Aphid' together with all-aspect capability and improved IRCM. It entered Soviet service in 1985 and has yet to be exported. The 'Archer' is known to exist in both IR- and radar-guided versions but, beyond the need for it to replace 'Aphid', little is known about the system.

The French Matra R550 Magic is probably the next most common dogfight missile. The widely exported Magic 1 version was used operationally during the Falklands conflict and the Iran–Iraq War. The improved Magic 2 offers some 10 per cent more motor thrust, thus greater range, and more effective fuzing. CATIC has produced a 'lookalike' missile, designated PL-7, while Armscor of South Africa offer the Kukri V3 and Darter missiles which bear a physical similarity to Magic.

The successor to Sidewinder in US and NATO service should have been the AIM-132 Advanced Short-Range AAM (ASRAAM) project, which came out of the 1980 MoU between Germany, the UK and United States. The UK and Germany were to develop ASRAAM, while the US continued with AMRAAM (now AIM-120) and, later, Norway and Canada became involved as sub-contractors. Delays, cost overruns and technical problems have blighted the project. By 1988 Norway, Canada and Germany had withdrawn, leaving British Aerospace Dynamics (BAeD) 'holding the baby'. The future of the project hinges on the selection of a contractor by the RAF. BAeD has since teamed with Hughes Aircraft of the United States to bid a re-worked AIM-132, while Marconi Defence Systems (MDS) of the UK has joined with Matra of France to offer a version of the latter's MICA (see below) known as MICASRAAM, using an MDS seeker, to the RAF. Raytheon, Loral (both from the United States) and Bodenseewerk Geratetechnik (BGT) of Germany have also expressed an interest in bidding.

If the Sidewinder has become the classic short-range dogfight missile, then the AIM-7 Sparrow series is its equivalent in the medium-range BVR category. Again, to chronicle the full developmental history of the AIM-7 would take a chapter on its own but for our purposes the AIM-7M is the starting point. Models up to the AIM-7F were equipped with progressively improved SAR guidance and remain in service worldwide. The AIM-7M has an inverse monopulse SAR seeker and, with digital data processing, offers a vastly improved ECCM capability. It also features an active-radar fuze with a more effective warhead. Raytheon acts as prime contractor and this company has been awarded an FSD contract for the AIM-7P model which is intended to provide a better performance against sea-skimming anti-ship missiles and cruise missiles.

The earlier AIM-7E-2 missile was taken as the starting point for a UK development from BAeD, now known as Sky Flash. The Sky Flash features a revised monopulse continuous-wave (CW) SAR seeker (from MDS) and a new fuze, autopilot and power supply unit, while later models have the Royal Ordnance Hoopoe rocket motor. Sky Flash is compatible with the AIM-7E used on RAF Phantoms and has been sold to Sweden as the Rb.71. Further proposed Swedish developments include an active-radar version (Rb.71a) and a ramjet-powered version (Rb.73) which is now on hold, following cost increases on the JAS.39 Gripen fighter programme. Active Sky Flash is a private venture between BAeD and Thomson-CSF, using a new active-radar seeker from Thomson. BAeD emphasizes that the active version is an export project only. Among the first potential customers could be Saudi Arabia (for Tornado F.53 fighters) and the Indian Navy, which is considering a similar mid-life update of its Sea Harriers to that under way in the RN's FRS.2 programme. MDS is also teamed with Dassault Electronique of France to develop an active-radar seeker for both AAMs and SAMs, and this seeker is being considered by Sweden for the Rb.71a programme.

In Italy, Selenia has developed the Sparrow into a family of shipborne, ground-based and airborne anti-aircraft missiles called Aspide. It features CW monopulse techniques and ECCM and HOJ capabilities. Shortly to enter service, it will arm the improved F-104ASA Starfighters of the Italian Air Force. It is thought that some components from the Aspide may have been sold to the PRC, which has developed an equivalent missile designated PL-9.

The US follow-up to AIM-7 is the AIM-120A AMRAAM, developed by Hughes Aircraft. A true 'fire-and-forget' missile, AIM-120 is slightly smaller than the Sparrow it will replace. The I-band seeker has a TWT amplifier, with variable PRF and frequency capabilities plus HOJ facilities. The missile is in the throes of final development – having experienced some production and fuze-arming problems. A number of models were deployed into the Gulf shortly before the end of hostili-

◄
The latest air-to-air missile in US service is the AIM-120A AMRAAM, seen here during trial firings from an F-15 Eagle. (Hughes Aircraft)

►
Displayed in front of the MiG-31 'Foxhound' at Le Bourget in 1991 are three major Soviet air-to-air missiles. A pair of Phoenix-lookalikes, AA-9 'Amos', are shown on the left, a pair of AA-8 'Aphids' to the centre and a single AA-6 'Acrid' to the rear. (Author)

ties, but they were not actually fired. Once the final problems are overcome, the USAF expects to procure 17,000 missiles and the US Navy some 7,000. In Europe, the RAF, the Fleet Air Arm and Germany's Luftwaffe are committed to procurement of the system. In the UK, it will arm Tornado F.3 and Sea Harrier FRS.2, while in Germany it will equip F-4 Phantoms being upgraded under the ICE programme. It was announced in June 1989 that MBB of Germany had been selected to lead the Euro-AMRAAM production, with BAeD of the UK and Raufoss of Norway as sub-contractors.

Always independent, France has developed the Matra R530/Super 530 system. The missile was initially developed in the late 1950s and the latest variant is the Super 530D, the development of which began in 1979. It features a CW SAR seeker with digital microprocessing for better ECCM capability. The company claims a maximum interception altitude of 80,000ft (24,400m) with a snap-up capability of 40,000ft (12,200m). The Super 530D entered L'Armée de l'Air Service on Mirage 2000s in 1987 and the whole family has been widely exported, seeing operational use in the Iran–Iraq War. Matra continued their AAM line in 1982, when they began the development of MICA (Missile d'Interception et de Combat Aérien) as a private venture. Interim development was approved by the French Government in 1985, with FSD authorized in 1987, looking towards an in-service date of 1995. The object of the programme is to produce a common missile with interchangeable IR- and active-radar guidance (using a Dassault Electronique AD 4A seeker). The latter option will include command updates and inertial guidance packages as well. The IR seeker will have the ability to lock on to targets either before or after launch. It will also feature common eject and rail-launcher interfaces with the Super 530 and Magic missiles.

The Soviet Union, again, has several missiles within this category: the AA-6 'Acrid' family, the AA-7 'Apex' and the AA-10 'Alamo' family. The last, using SAR guidance, is available in both medium-range and long-range versions and arms the Su-27 'Flanker'. Apart from the long-range 'Alamo', the other main long-range BVR missile on the Soviet inventory is the AA-9 'Amos', which was first identified arming the MiG-31 'Foxhound' in 1985 and shown in the West for the first time at Le Bourget in 1991. Bearing a striking resemblance to the US AIM-54 Phoenix, it is available in two versions, with either SAR or inertial/active-radar guidance. A version with a passive anti-radar seeker, for use against NATO AEW aircraft, is also thought to be under development.

Development of the Hughes AIM-54 Phoenix began in 1960. Initially intended to arm the cancelled F-111B, the system was carried over to its successor, the F-14 Tomcat. Production of the analogue AIM-54A ceased in 1980, after the missile was effectively compromised following the Iranian Revolution. Tomcats were supplied to the Shah's régime, complete with AIM-54A missiles, and several examples of the latter are understood to have found their way to the Soviet Union. The digital AIM-54C follow-on offers several improvements over the A model, including active terminal guidance, inertial mid-course guidance, improved ECCM and an active-radar fuze. Deliveries of the AIM-54C+, with specific reliability improvements, began in 1986.

For the future, US Navy studies of the outer air battle have led to a requirement for an Advanced AAM

(AAAM), smaller than the Phoenix but with an improved performance. A four-year competitive demonstration and validation phase began in October 1988, with contracts let to two competing teams – General Dynamics' Pomona Division/Westinghouse and Hughes Aircraft/Raytheon, with McDonnell Douglas Missiles, Marquardt and the Hercules Corporation as sub-contractors. Details of the individual designs are sketchy as yet, and the outcome of the programme is unpredictable.

Air-to-Ground Weapons

The bomb is the oldest form of air-delivered weapon and its design has come a long way since intrepid aviators pulled pins out of Mills bombs (or other hand grenades), dropped them over the side of a BE.2c and hoped for the best. While the conventional, high-explosive, free-fall bomb which evolved through two world wars is still with us, the variations on that theme are legion. They can be dispensed from bomb-like cases or purpose-built dispensers, they can be retarded by airbrakes or parachutes and they can have rocket-propelled penetrators which can pierce concrete.

The basic technology involved in such weapons, however, has hardly changed since 1918. The high-explosive (HE), general-purpose (GP) bomb has only become more streamlined (to allow external carriage on modern fast-jet combat aircraft) and more reliable. Practically all the bombs dropped during the Falklands conflict of 1982 were of immediate postwar vintage and the only major shortcoming revealed was the need for faster fuzing systems so that when they are dropped at low level (down to 50ft) at speeds of up to 500kts they are ready to detonate on impact with the target. Older bombs can be, and are now being, updated by the addition of more sophisticated and reliable fuzes. How many more ships would the Royal Navy have lost had such fuzes been available to the Argentine Air Force in 1982?

If one was to categorize today's bombs (discounting those with NBC or FAE warheads), three major divisions appear: the conventional HE GP bomb, the cluster bomb and the area-denial bomb. Within the first category, sub-divisions of free-fall, retarded and laser-guided (non-powered and powered) appear; while for the last two categories there are various systems, leading up to the weapons dispenser system (WDS). The WDS, while using bomblets or submunitions, is not, in itself, a bomb in the conventional sense.

Following the shooting down of Gary Powers's U-2 reconnaissance aircraft by a Soviet SA-2 'Guideline' SAM in 1960, it became obvious that strike aircraft would have to reduce their penetration and delivery altitude to attack targets. This meant that the air crewmen had less time to line up their target to ensure the accurate delivery of their bombs. The 'shotgun' principle was then considered, by which more smaller bombs would stand a better chance of hitting the target than one larger one, thus compensating for the lack of aiming time. In some ways this was a return to the thinking of the interwar years. However, it saw two major developments – the so-called Mk. 80 series of 'slick' bombs developed in the United States and elsewhere and the cluster bomb and subsequent area munition systems.

As release speeds became higher, faster-arming fuzes were developed, mounted either in the nose or tail of these systems and with degrees of initiation ranging from basic impact to timed-delays for air-burst effect. Care must be taken, however, not to allow bombs to arm themselves too quickly after release. During the Vietnam War the US forces soon discovered that releasing bombs in clutches (for the 'shotgun' effect) could also back-fire on the strike aircraft releasing them: rapidly armed weapons frequently knocked against each other and, with impact fuzes, this led to instances of bombs exploding as near as 50ft (15m) below the releasing aircraft. Partly as a way of overcoming this situation with conventional bombs, the technique for delivering smaller nuclear weapons, known as toss-bombing, was adapted for conventional use. In either case, the strike aircraft penetrates enemy territory at low altitude, so as to avoid radar detection, and just short of the target pulls up into a vertical climb. The bombs are released at the correct angle, enabling them to climb under their own kinetic energy over a ballistic arc, falling down on to the target. Meanwhile the aircraft continues over the top of a loop and executes a roll-over manœuvre (basically a half-Cuban Eight), placing itself on the reciprocal course to that of the bomb and thus escaping bomb blast.

The alternative to toss-bombing was the exact opposite of the concept of the low-drag bomb – retardation by various means. Slowing the bomb down enabled the aircraft to get clear of the impact area. However, as bombs needed to be low-drag for external carriage, retarding systems which activated after release were developed. In the United States the Snakeye system of metal high-drag retarders was mounted on the tail section of the bomb, between the fins, opening umbrella-like to slow it down; when applied to the Mk. 81/82 bombs, these became Snakeye Mod. 1 bombs. In the UK, Hunting Engineering developed the Type 117 and 118 retarded tails, with four airbrake panels linked by drag ribbons. The classic airborne retarder, the parachute, was also adapted for installation in bomb tail units. These are available for a wide variety of ordnance. A variation on the theme is the US Goodyear-developed BSU-49/B 'ballute' or balloon parachute. The ballute is housed in the tail unit and deploys after release. Four air scoops in the 'bag' rapidly inflate the ballute and an effective braking system is provided.

So much for the 'shotgun' approach to delivering bombs on to targets. As we have noted, it is a very old concept brought up to date. What air forces appreciate today is accurate delivery, demonstrated to effect on our television screens during the Gulf War. They can, of course, use air-to-surface missiles but these tend to be expensive and only limited numbers are likely to be afforded by the majority of air forces. Far better would be a way of guiding the GP bomb on to the target with a similar accuracy under the power of gravity. Enter the 'smart' bomb.

Again, the needs of Vietnam operations spurred developments, and in April 1965 the first laser-guided bomb (LGB), developed under the Paveway programme by the US Armament Development and Test Center at Eglin AFB, in collaboration with Texas Instruments, was dropped. A family of laser-guidance units was developed as the Paveway I, which could be fitted to six main types of bomb in the Mk. 80 series. The beauty of the LGBs was that they required no airframe or electrical modification and they could be treated just like any other free-fall bomb as regards storage and loading on to aircraft. Existing bombs can be converted to LGB configuration by fitting a guidance unit on the nose and enlarged tailfins. The common guidance unit is mounted on the nose in a universally jointed, free housing with an annular tail ring. The silicon detector array is divided into four quadrants which send signals to the guidance computer, which, in turn, drives the four control fins. The sensor is kept pointing at the target source of laser illumination and, as both theory suggests and much practice has proved, the bomb will impact on the same point.

All this, of course, presupposes that the target is marked by a laser designator, either in the air on the launch aircraft or his wingman, or by ground-based designators operated by forward troops. Once illuminated, the spot where the laser hits the target reflects the laser radiation, which is detected by the LGB of laser-homing missile. The homing head then measures the angle between the longitudinal axis of the missile and the missile-to-target line, automatically guiding the missile to the centre of the laser spot. Current airborne laser designator pods in service and/or under development include the Thomson-CSF Atlis II, Westinghouse Pave Spike, Hughes Aircraft TRAM, Martin Marietta LANTIRN and GEC-Ferranti TIALD, all of which were used during the Gulf War.

The Paveway system has been widely sold, to seventeen countries in all. The latest Paveway III system, which is just coming into US service, has microprocessor control and flip-out wings and can be dropped at very low altitude. The digital autopilot uses a BAeD Dart precision gyro, enabling operation in poor visibility with a low cloudbase. The system can also now be delivered in the dive, from level flight or in a toss manœuvre. A major competitor to the Paveway is the French LGB, developed by SAMP and Matra in collaboration with Thomson-CSF. Designed for use with Atlis II designator pods, this can also be used with Ferranti and Hughes Aircraft laser systems. The nose guidance is based on Paveway, but with modifications to the guidance vanes, and, together with the flip-out fins, can be readily fitted to existing conventional HE bombs.

▶ Typical of the laser-guided bomb is this 1,000kg LGB from Matra Defence of France, seen here launched from a Mirage 2000. (Matra Defence)

▼ Laser-guided weapons of all types depend on designation of some description. This simple diagram illustrates the co-operative designation provided by a TIALD-carrying Tornado for the weapon dropped by a second aircraft. (GEC-Ferranti)

Another Vietnam-era development for 'smart' bombs was the TV-homing Pave Strike HOBOS (homing-bomb system), of which the GBU-8 was the main production model. In essence, an electro-optical (TV-type) seeker, body strakes and controllable fins were fitted to a Mk. 84 bomb. Sensor information was sent back to the launch aircraft by data link and the weapons system operator (WSO) in the back seat steered the bomb on to the target. Its successor is Rockwell International's GBU-15 cruciform wing weapon (CWW), again based on the Mk. 84 bomb (but there is also a version using the CBU-75 cluster bomb). It uses TV or imaging IR sensors and, after launch, while the delivery aircraft is flying away from the target, the data link allows the WSO to steer the weapon to the general target area, whereupon the weapon climbs until it can acquire the target and then dives upon it. The WSO has the option of steering the weapon all the way to the target or locking-in the homing head.

With such homing systems applied to free-fall LGBs, it was but a short step to investigate the addition of a propulsive system to endow the bomb with a stand-off range. From the Paveway, Emerson Electric developed the AGM-123 Skipper and from the GBU-15 Rockwell developed the AGM-130A system. However, once the motor has been added, such systems become, to all intents and purposes, air-to-surface missiles (witness the US 'AGM' designations) and are covered later in this chapter.

The need to ensure that bombs reached and destroyed their targets led to the reconsideration of the 'shotgun' principle, not only with regard to releasing more, smaller GP bombs but also centred on the fragmentation effect caused by the shattering of the HE GP bomb casings. The pattern of metal shards or shrapnel produced is lethal against unprotected personnel and can severely damage soft-skinned targets. In an effort to increase the kill probability and counter enemy superiority, this fragmentation effect was refined to produce what is today known as the cluster bomb. The basic principle here is that an outer, streamlined casing contains a number of small submunitions. An advantage of the cluster bomb is that it exhibits the same basic flight characteristics as a GP bomb and so can be launched in a toss-bombing manœuvre. After bomb release, a timing device initiates the release of the whole or part of the outer casing, which in turn allows the submunitions to fall away by gravity.

The UK's Improved BL755 system, from Hunting Engineering, uses a small parachute to give a greater angle-of-attack and a hot gas cartridge to initiate the split-away of the casing, the slipstream completing the removal. Once this is accomplished, a second cartridge begins to inflate a bladder inside the core of the submunition clusters to expel them from the casing. Seven bays within the body each carry 21 bomblets (a total of 147), and the ejection velocity is varied to ensure an even ground pattern. Improvements in explosives and shaped-charge technology have increased the weapon's effectiveness against armour. Being involved in both BL755 and the lay-down JP233 dispenser, Hunting have seen the advantages of both systems and developed an air-delivered solution to the attack and closure of high-value fixed targets and choke points. The Hunting Area Denial System (HADES) combines the proven BL755 dispenser body with 49 Ferranti HB876 area-denial submunitions.

In US cluster bombs, the separation method involves a detonating cord blowing away the casing. The consequent spread of these submunitions depends on the number contained and the height at which they are released. The large numbers of US cluster bomb units (CBUs) are based on a dispenser, designated SUU (suspended underwing unit), with the appropriate bomb live unit (BLU) submunition installed. The combinations are apparently endless, although the principal system is the Rockeye II Mk. 20 (CBU-59/B), which dispenses 247 dual-purpose, shaped-charge bomblets. When released from 500ft (152m), a typical dispersal pattern of 51,667 sq. ft. (4,800m^2) is achieved. Similar in size to a conventional 500lb (228kg) GP bomb, Rockeye was also used with success during the Gulf War.

The CBU-87/B system, produced by Aerojet Ordnance, has been described to the author as 'the last of the dumb bombs'. The shaped charge of the bomblet is backed up by an incendiary element and a very long fragmentation coil producing 30-grain fragments. This is as sophisticated as possible without resorting to smart munitions. After release, at altitudes down to 200ft (61m) and speeds up to 700kts, the CEM's tailfins spin up the dispenser (to a maximum of 2,500rpm) and the body skins are released. There is in-flight selection of the height of the burst. On encountering the airstream, the submunitions deploy their decelerator, stabilize and are armed. Although effective results are claimed, no figures are available for dispersal patterns.

The latest ISC Technologies product to enter US inventories is the ISCB-1 area-denial cluster weapon. Based on Rockeye, it uses computer techniques to achieve an air-delivered fragmentation with variable programmed detonation of individual area-denial mines. The weapon consists of the Mk. 7 dispenser, a Mk. 339 nose fuze, a tail cone assembly and 160 electronically timed mines (pre-set on the ground) plus 65 decoy mines. Depending on the release altitude, an area of between 32,230 sq. ft. (3,000m^2) and 53,820 sq. ft. (5,000m^2) can be covered.

The principal cluster weapon in service with the French is the Matra/Thomson-Brandt Belouga system. Of low-drag configuration, this 672lb (305kg) weapon disperses 151×66mm grenades each weighing 2.9lb (1.3kg) in a regular pattern. Three main types of grenade have been developed: a general-purpose or fragmentation round, for soft-skinned targets, parked aircraft or fuel stores; an armour-piercing round for use against armoured vehicles of all descriptions; and an area interdiction round for communications infrastructures. The typical area coverage of the weapon is an ellipse some 130–200ft (40–60m) wide and 390–780ft (120–240m) long. The pilot may select either of two pattern configurations prior to release.

Always known for innovative development, Israel's Rafael has produced a more conventional cluster bomb known as TAL. The TAL-1 is designed to produce a high rate of spin, so that the submunition bomblets will be scattered over a wide area in a circular pattern. Although starved of Western techology, both Chile and South Africa are still capable of developing modern systems, and Cardoen and Armscor respectively include cluster bombs in their ranges of products. The Spanish BME 330 cluster bomb, in production at Expal Explosives Alaveses, contains 180 bomblets of three

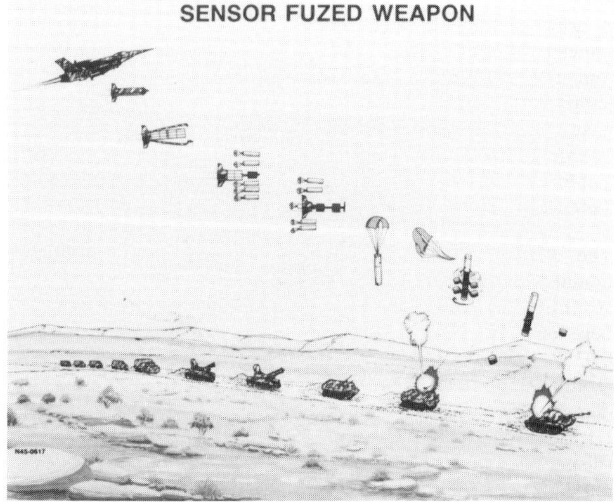

types, depending on role: an anti-personnel round using a fragmentation case; an incendiary version; and a hollow-charge warhead. The Soviet Union has had cluster bombs of various types in service for several years. Exact details have not been released but HE, incendiary, HEI, fragmentation and anti-armour (with a shaped-charge warhead) types are known to exist.

The reorganization of aircraft dispersal sites by the introduction of hardened aircraft shelters (HAS) means that the most vulnerable target on an airfield is now the runway itself. Initially one-shot runway-denial weapons of traditional 'bomb' size were developed. Matra's Durandal must be the classic weapon of the genre: it is a refined version of the concepts developed by France and Israel for the so-called 'concrete dibber' bomb of the 1967 Arab–Israeli War. Despite its trials and export success (having been sold to the USAF), Durandal was not adapted by France itself. Instead of Durandal, the French Air Force preferred the Thomson-Brandt BAP (Bombe d'Appui Pénétration) 100 area-denial and cratering system. It is actually half-way between the cluster bomb and dispenser system, being slightly smaller than the Mk. 82 bomb, and it is carried in clusters of eighteen per aircraft. The manufacturers claim that BAP 100 requires the release of 12–18 weapons (dependent on the aircraft sighting system) to achieve a runway 'cut' at low altitude and high speed. After release, a brake parachute stabilizes the weapon, whereupon a rocket motor is ignited to ensure concrete penetration and, after the optimum delay, the warhead is exploded. The BAP 100 was used operationally by French Jaguars in their successful attack on the Ouadi Doum in Chad in February 1986. A derivative system, the BAT (Bombe d'Appui Tactique) 120, is designed to engage surface targets such as soft-skinned convoys, missile sites and parked aircraft.

Currently under development in the United States is the Direct Airfield Attack Combined Munition (DAACM), a package comprising eight Textron Defense Systems BLU-106/B Boosted Kinetic Energy Penetrators (BKEP) and 24 Hunting Engineering HB876 area-denial mines (as used in JP233) in the Ferranti SUU-64/B Tactical Munitions Dispenser (TMD). The BKEP craters the runway by using a parachute to stabilize the munition to an angle of 65 degrees, when a rocket motor ignites and causes the weapon to penetrate the surface. Detonation follows penetration. Also under development by Textron Defense Systems for the USAF Armament Division at Eglin AFB is the Sensor Fuzed Weapon (SFW). This uses ten BLU-108/B submunitions carried in the SUU-64/B TMD, each BLU-108/B carrying four Textron Defense Systems Skeet (TM) smart anti-armour warheads. The SFW can be used from high altitude or on low-level, high-speed runs to attack both column or array targets. The SFW is also capable of being released by toss-bombing techniques to achieve a stand-off distance. Once the submunitions are released and the stabilizing parachute has done its job, the four Skeet (TM) warheads are thrown outwards and upwards in search of targets over a large area. The built-in sensor in each warhead finds a target and fires an Explosively Formed Penetrator

◀ A drawing showing both the concept of the cluster bomb and the application of the smart submunition, in this case the Sensor Fuzed Weapon, using the Textron Defense Skeet. (Textron Defense)

▶ The British JP233 airfield-denial weapon system from Hunting Engineering, seen here on trials, uses the RO SG357 cratering munition (coming from the rear of the dispenser) and the Ferranti HB756 area-denial weapon (dispensed from the front part). (Hunting Engineering)

(EFP) into the vulnerable topside area of the AFV. In two specific tests, Textron Defense claims that four Skeets from a single BLU-108/B submunition scored hits on four separate tanks.

Area-denial systems get more complex than cluster bombs when lay-down systems such as the UK's JP233 and Germany's MW-1 are considered. For counter-air operations, the RAF uses Hunting Engineering's JP233 dispenser system in the airfield attack role. Its use during the Gulf War was at the specific request of the US military commander. JP233 is a system designed specifically for paired carriage by Tornado GR.1s. In a high-speed, low-level delivery, it lays down two complementary submunitions: the Royal Ordnance SG357 cratering weapon, to attack and render unusable runways, taxiways and grass airstrips, and the Ferranti HB876 area-denial weapon, to pose a threat to vehicles and troops engaged in airfield repair. Each JP233 weapon consists of 30 SG357 submunitions in the aft bay and 215 HB876 mines in the forward way. Both types of submunitions are dispensed simultaneously.

Using the expertise gained from JP233, Hunting has now developed a new cratering munitions dispenser known as CMD18. Designed for the SG357 cratering submunition of JP233 (in the same way that HADES was developed for the HB876), the flexible design concept allows the weapon to be configured for a variety of aircraft types. Carrying eighteen SG357 submunitions and used in conjunction with HADES, it offers a JP233 capability for attack aircraft smaller than Tornado.

An equivalent to JP233 developed by Raketen Technik GmbH (RTG), a subsidiary of MBB and Diehl, is known as MW-1. This conventional multi-purpose dispenser weapon system is intended for use against airfields and mechanized armoured units, whether in battle, in transit or marshalling. Specifically designed for carriage by the Tornado, it is mounted on the aircraft centreline and ejects its submunitions sideways. The coverage of the system (known as 'pattern length') is crew-controlled, while the pattern width is achieved through submunition-defined ejection speeds. It can be used in all weathers, day or night. Five types of submunition are available, covering both active and passive systems.

A derivative of MW-1, known as the Modular Dispenser System (MDS), has been developed by MBB for tactical attack aircraft other than the Tornado. Sweden has ordered a stand-off, dropped-container variant known as the Dispenser Weapons System (DWS) 39 from that company for its JAS.39 Gripen. Similar in nature to MW-1 and MDS, DWS-39 can be configured for use on almost any tactical aircraft and for most operational functions. It can have a length of between 8.2ft (2.5m) and 14.8ft (4.5m) and weigh between 1,100lb (500kg) and 4,400lb (2,000kg), the submunitions comprising between 70 and 80 per cent of those weights.

Another German system is the Vertical Ballistic Weapon (VBW), from MBB. Mounted in a reusable pod are eighteen munition-launch tubes and a variety of sensors that scan the ground as it is overflown. Once a target (an AFV for preference) has been sensed, then the eighteen bazooka-type weapons (which are pointed aft through the pod) are launched. Weighing only 705lb (320kg) and being some 13ft (4m) long, the VBW pod can be carried in pairs by an aircraft as small as the Alpha Jet or Hawk.

Alkan and Lacroix of France build a much less complex and low-cost system for dispensing 74mm grenades (sometimes known as 'cartridges'), mounted either internally within the aircraft or externally on a stores pylon. The grenades used are the Lacroix CAV.314, weighing 6.6lb (3kg), for fragmentation (with a fuze delay, allowing detonation on the rebound), and

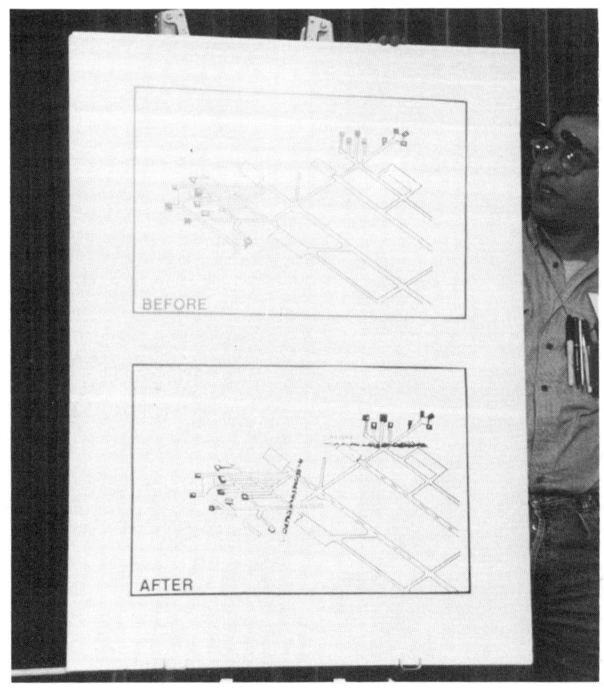

the Thomson-Brandt grenade, using a hollow-charge warhead which, the company claims, can penetrate 230mm of steel. Although the weapon is dispensed vertically, released when the aircraft is diving at a relatively shallow angle of 20 degrees, the width of coverage can be increased. These systems can be used at speeds of up to 600kts and from altitudes as low as 100ft (30m).

The Italian consortium of CASMU (Alenia and SNIA-BPD) is developing the Skyshark stand-off weapons dispenser for the Tornado and AMX strike aircraft. Presently unpowered, it has a glide range of some 6–12km, although a rocket-powered version is planned which will take the range out to 20–25km. The submunitions are ejected sideways, as in MW-1. Weighing some 1,642lb (745kg), the basic 'gliding' version can be released at speeds of between 500 and 550kts.

The airborne weapons dispenser system, in all shapes and sizes, has been amply demonstrated and, obviously, the stand-off mode is preferred, especially in the light of recent operational experience. Following the débâcles of the collaborative LR-SOM (Long-Range Stand-Off Missile), LOCPOD (Low-Cost, Powered, Off-boresight Dispenser) and MSOW (Modular Stand-Off Weapon) systems during the 1980s, individual nations are looking anew at stand-off weapons, some having dispenser systems. The various countries are now considering their options in the light of experience and the reduced need for such a weapon in Central Europe. The United States is considering a development from Brunswick Defense, based on the LAD, known as LOCLAD (Low Cost, Low Altitude Dispenser). This offers day/night area targeting, ranges of up to 20nm (37km) and release altitudes down to 100ft (30m). British Aerospace, working for the Aerospace Division of the UK's Defence Research Agency (DRA – formerly the Royal Aerospace Establishment), is developing the REVISE (Research Vehicle for In-flight Submunition Ejection) weapon. This is part of a BAe-DRA joint venture aimed at creating a stand-off weapon for use by RAF Tornados. From REVISE work, BAe is developing MANTIS (Man-in-the-loop Tactical Interdiction System) and AUTIS (Autonomous Tactical Interdiction System), stand-off weapons for attacking hardened aircraft shelters and 'soft' targets.

Following their withdrawal from MSOW, the French proceeded independently with a development of the powered Apache system for L'Armée de l'Air, with Matra and Aérospatiale working together. Apache is a modular system some 14ft 5in (4.4m) long and weigh-

◀ The effectiveness of JP233 during the Gulf War is seen in these two drawings of its use shown to the world's press early in the confict. (US DoD)

▶ A new US submunition dispenser weapon is the Low Cost, Low Altitude Dispenser (LOCLAD) from Brunswick Defense, seen here under the wing of a trials F-16. (Brunswick Defense)

◀ Another new concept, from Rockwell International, is the Low Cost Advanced Technology Missile (LOCATM). The missile, carried in three-, four- or six-packs, has a triangular shape and folding control surfaces and features low drag and low-radar-observable design. (Rockwell)

▶ This view of the Westland-built S-70 Black Hawk helicopter during weapons trials illustrates the use of 2.75in aerial rockets in the ground-attack role. (Westlands)

ing 2,650lb (1,200kg). The four modules comprise the nose section, containing guidance, control and navigation equipment; the hardback (or spine), providing interfacing with the carrier aircraft and operating systems related to wing-deployment after release; the payload section, for interchangeable magazines with either sideways or axial submunition ejection; and the tail section, with wing-shaped stabilizers, the jet engine and fuel tank. The range of submunitions consists of the Mimosa general-purpose munition, the Arcadie semi-intelligent, anti-armour submunition (under pre-development) and the Kriss anti-runway submunition, the last-named announced just after Le Bourget in 1991.

Seen as the crossover point between 'dumb' and guided weapons, the airborne weapon dispenser system is like Falstaff's Otter – 'neither fish nor flesh'. However, unlike the Shakespearian text, the man (in this case, the air forces of five nations) does know where to 'have her' – on their inventories as a conventional weapon 'force-multiplier'. Such systems are becoming increasingly popular, particularly where a stand-off capability is required.

Before moving on to dedicated air-to-ground missiles, mention must be made of the current version of the air-to-ground, unguided rocket, principally for use against armour, concentrations of softer-skinned vehicles or large point targets. The ungainly 'large firework' concept of rocket projectile in service at the end of the Second World War has now been replaced by smaller, more compact systems either carried in an aerodynamic pod (which may be jettisoned after use) or mounted in vertical banks. The former type, known as folding-fin aerial rockets (FFAR), are typified by the Matra 68mm SNEB and Hughes 2.75in systems, are for faster combat aircraft, while the latter, such as Forge

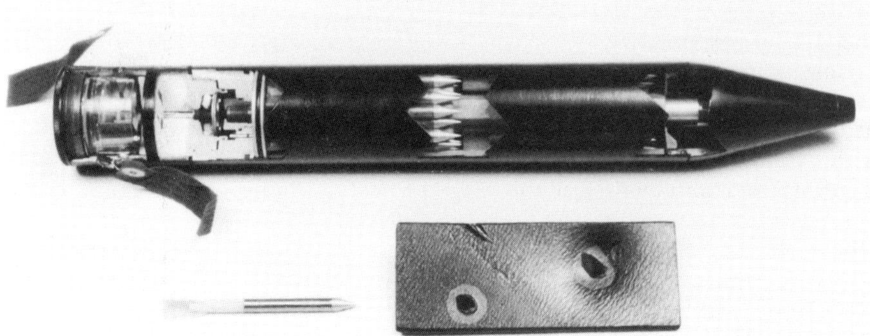

◀ An example of how submunition technology is applied to aerial rockets is this 68mm 'warhead' with penetrator darts for use against light armoured vehicles, developed by Thomson Brandt Armements of France. (TBA)

de Zeebrugge's 80mm and 81mm SNORA rockets, can be fitted to slower, armed trainers or helicopters. Even the submunition concept can be applied to such apparently simple weapons. Thomson-Brandt of France has developed a 'multi-dart' flechette system whereby three or more (depending on the calibre of the rocket) such projectiles are deployed once the rocket is well down its trajectory. This increases the area effect of the rocket as a weapons system. SNIA-BPD of Italy has also developed a submunition package for its 81mm BPD rocket in the form of eleven AT-AP warheads.

The Gulf War saw the operational début of a Canadian product – the CRV-7 2.75in rocket developed by Bristol Aerospace. The RAF made a rush purchase of sufficient systems to equip the squadron of Jaguar GR.1As deployed to the Gulf in late 1990. Each Jaguar was able to carry two 19-round launchers. After a false start, before the software for computed weapon-aiming became available, the CRV-7s were achieving more than acceptable results. Whether the system remains on the RAF inventory is now a matter for evaluation.

The subject of true air-to-ground missiles is a large one, covering anti-tank guided weapons (ATGWs), 'general-purpose' missiles with various targeting seekers, anti-radiation missiles (ARMs) and both tactical and strategic nuclear missiles. Space does not allow the inclusion of every type, so the reader mut accept a representative selection to illustrate emerging capabilities. The Hughes AGM-65 Maverick series typifies the current range of air-to-ground missiles (AGMs) and is produced in several variants: the AGM-65A and B represent the basic TV-guided model, while the original laser-guided version, the C, was cancelled in favour of the less-expensive E model; the D model is the USAF's imaging-IR (IIR) version for night and all-weather attack; the US Navy Maverick, the F model, combines the IIR seeker of the D with the warhead and propulsion system of the E model; and the G model is the USAF version of the F. The USAF is investigating the integration of a passive radar seeker with the A model TV-guidance under the 'Have Wedge' programme. Another important US system is the Rockwell International AGM-130. This is a rocket-powered version of the GBU-15 guided bomb mentioned earlier, available in three variants: the A model, based on the 2,000lb Mk. 84 bomb; the B, based on the SUU-54 airfield-attack submunition dispenser and carrying fifteen boosted kinetic energy penetrators and 75 Ferranti HB876 area-denial submunitions as used on the RAF's JP233 system; and the C model, carrying a 2,000lb BLU-109/B penetrating warhead.

The UK has a requirement, SR(A).1238, for an unpowered, steerable dispenser for anti-armour submunitions for use by the Harrier GR.5/7 force. In order to make maximum use of the weapons, a high kill rate per pass and hence per sortie is required – somewhere in the region of 8–11 tank kills per sortie. Although still on the RAF's 'wish list', it is currently 'on ice' because of a lack of funds. Up to 1990, two teams had been selected with a view to evaluating their offerings: Marconi Defence Systems, with a version of the Rockwell International AGM-114 Hellfire missile known as Brimstone; and Hunting Engineering, offering a compliant

◄
The interdictor version of the Eagle, the F-15E, is seen here launching an AGM-65B Maverick air-to-ground missile during integration trials. Maverick was used with great success during the Gulf War and exists in several variants. (Hughes Aircraft)

►
Derived from the Harpoon anti-ship missile, the AGM-84E SLAM (Stand-off Land Attack Missile) made its successful début during the Gulf War, launched from a variety of US Navy aircraft including the F/A-18 Hornet illustrated. (McDonnell Douglas Missiles)

◄
Under evaluation by the US Navy is the Advanced Interdiction Weapon System (AIWS) from the team of Texas Instruments and LTV. A flight test of the missile from an F-4 Phantom has been successfully completed. (Texas Instruments)

bid and, teamed with Honeywell of the US, the non-compliant SWAARM (Smart Weapon Anti-Armour). The Marconi Defence Systems proposal sees a new millimetric-wave seeker mated to the Hellfire missile. Brimstone would be carried in clusters of four from the aircraft's pylons for independent launch as targets were acquired. SWAARM is an unpowered, steered dispenser containing sixteen sensor-fuzed munitions, derived from the Alliant Techsystems SADARM (Sense and Destroy Armour) programme. Diehl of Germany is supporting Alliant in the development of the explosively formed projectile which is fired from the munition after target acquisition and identification. The weapon itself is relased at very low level and, after safe separation, climbs before releasing the munitions. These descend by parachute, using the vortex-ring effect to allow the IR and millimetre-wave radar sensors in the store to scan the area beneath in a search for armoured targets during descent. It is not known if the submunitions can be individually targeted. Being a line-of-sight, stand-off weapon, SWAARM can use standard targeting systems. According to Hunting, it is capable of achieving multiple kills in a single pass by the attacking aircraft.

From France comes the Aérospatiale AS.30L laser-guided missile, which was used in the Gulf War to great effect. Carried by French Jaguars, it provided an accurate, stand-off capability against heavily defended and hardened targets. Unlike Maverick, which coasts to the target after initial rocket-burn, AS.30L is powered all the way to the target, impacting at around Mach 1.4 and offering tremendous kinetic energy to its 'punch' in addition to its warhead. An Aérospatiale spokesman told the author that although the weapon was expensive it did offer value for money with a high probability of success. Aérospatiale also has the ASMP (Air-Sol Moyen Portée) nuclear-armed short-range cruise missile in service with the Mirage IVP and Mirage 2000N, replacing a free-fall tactical weapon, while at Le Bourget in 1991 the company revealed the follow-on ASLP (Air-Sol Longue Portée) long-range successor to ASMP, for use on the Rafale.

The United States has three other major projects. Boeing Aerospace is developing the SRAM (Short-Range Attack Missile) II to replace the existing AGM-69A SRAM (since cancelled by President Bush in late 1991) and, under a USAF contract, LTV are developing a Hypervelocity Missile which kills tanks by its sheer speed of impact – 1.5km/sec. McDonnell Douglas has taken its Harpoon anti-ship missile and developed it as a Stand-off Land Attack Missile (SLAM) for the US Navy. Designated AGM-84E, this was yet another 'smart' weapon used to effect during the Gulf War.

The US Navy is now looking to its next generation stand-off weapon, the Advanced Interdiction Weapons System (AIWS), designed to replace the Walleye TV-guided bomb, the AGM-123 Skipper, the AGM-65 Maverick and the laser-guided bomb. It must be compatible with current and planned systems, have a stand-off capability outside point defences and be effective against area and point targets (and hit them); fundamentally, it must be affordable, with a target cost of $50,000 per weapon. It will achieve its stand-off range from a high-lift, low-drag airframe and be flexible enough to be launched from either high or low altitude. It will use precise navigation and will have the option of a single or submunition warhead. Texas Instruments and LTV's Missiles Division have combined to form one of the teams investigating AIWS, which is more like a UAV than a missile.

Missiles specifically designed to home on radar transmissions – anti-radiation missiles (ARMs) – were also used during the Gulf War. The Texas Instruments AGM-88A Harm (High-speed ARM) is the current production type. Motorola are also currently rebuilding obsolete AIM-9C Sidewinder AAMs as the AGM-122 Sidearm to enable AV-8 and AH-1 aircraft to have an ARM capability.

The British Alarm (Air-Launched ARM), from British Aerospace Dynamics, was rushed into production for the Gulf War and was deemed very successful. Unlike the US Harm, which is a point-and-shoot weapon, Alarm is intended for carefully pre-planned defence-suppression missions. It is a loitering missile. On launch, it climbs to about 70,000ft, where it deploys a parachute and descends slowly. If the enemy radar is switched on, the parachute is jettisoned and the missile is projected to its target. If no emissions are detected, then the missile will eventually explode harmlessly in the desert (or wherever), the effect of keeping radars switched off having been achieved. In all, 121 Alarms were fired before stocks were exhausted. Its effectiveness will ensure its inclusion in the RAF's armoury for many years ahead.

In anti-surface vessel warfare, the anti-ship missile (ASM) has proved its effectiveness operationally. It would be a fair statement to make that many ASMs launched from either fixed-wing aircraft or helicopters are derivatives of naval (i.e. surface- or ship-launched) ASMs, although some of the smaller ones, like BAeD's Sea Skua and the Aérospatiale AS.15TT, were specifically designed as helicopter systems. They basically operate by being given target co-ordinates from the launch aircraft or helicopter and then pursuing a sea-skimming mode (using a radar altimeter) until the missile seeker picks up the target. Some longer-range systems have a facility for mid-course guidance. Again, just a representative selection will be described here.

Sea Skua, four of which can be carried by the Lynx, was combat-proven in both the 1982 Falklands conflict and the 1991 Gulf War. The effectiveness of this system against the smaller vessels of the Iraqi Navy was devastating. The AS.15TT was developed for use by the Saudi Arabian Navy from their SA.365F Dauphins as part of the 'Sawari' frigate programme. Like Sea Skua, these missiles were equally effective against Iraqi craft in their operational début. At the larger end of the scale, Aérospatiale's AM.39 version of Exocet hit the headlines during the Falklands campaign and is currently in service with thirteen nations using both fixed- and rotary-wing craft as platforms. From BAeD is the Sea Eagle, which is now in RAF service on board the Buccaneer S.2A/B, and is to be transferred to the Tornado by 1993. It has also been adapted for operation by the Sea King Mk. 42B now being built for the Indian Navy. The McDonnell Douglas AGM-84A Harpoon, the standard US anti-ship missile, also saw operational success when, in March 1986, A-6 Intruders of the US Sixth Fleet launched them against Libyan 'Nanuchka' class guided-missile corvettes, scoring at least one hit. Production of all variants of Harpoon has now exceeded 4,000, and the current version in production is the Block 1D missile with additional fuel capacity (as well as a switch from JP-5 to JP-10), an increased computer memory and an improved seeker.

Among other countries with developed ASMs are China, which fields the CATIC C601, two of which are carried by its H-6 (Tu-16) bombers. It is a low-level sea-skimmer, using a monopulse radar seeker. MBB of West Germany has produced the Kormoran, which is in service with the Marineflieger and on order for Italian Tornados. The Mk. 2 will be used by German Tornados. MBB and Aérospatiale are currently collaborating on an Exocet and Kormoran successor, known as the Anti-Navire Supersonique (ANS), with an in-service date set for the mid-1990s. ANS is powered by a unique rocket-ramjet motor and will be capable of defensive manœuvres. Israel has developed an air-launched version of Gabriel Mk. III, and progress on the air-breathing Mk. IV has yet to be reported. Current intelligence does not credit the Soviet Union with any equivalent of the 'traditional' Exocet or Harpoon type of ASM. It is known, however, that the AS-4 'Kitchen', AS-6 'Kingfisher' and AS-7 'Kerry' can be used against shipping.

Continuing development has seen the Norsk Forsvartsteknologi Penguin adopted for use by the US Navy on its SH-60B Seahawk LAMPS III helicopters in Mk. 2 Mod. 7 form. Some 200 are on order, and Grumman Aerospace will build them in the United States. This version is also being cleared for use by the naval variant of the Westland Lynx. The Penguin Mk. 3 (US designation AGM-119) is being developed as part of the Operation Capability Update for Norwegian F-16s, and the USAF is showing interest itself. Another Nordic company, Saab Missiles of Sweden, has, in collaboration with Bofors, developed the RBS.15F. It lacks the

◀ Another new weapon rushed into service during the Gulf War was the BAeD Air-Launched Anti-Radar Missile (Alarm), two of which can be seen under the fuselage of this Tornado GR.1. (BAe Military Aircraft)

▶ The Penguin anti-ship missile, developed by NFT of Norway and sold to the US Navy, is available in both Mk. 2 and Mod. 7 helicopter-launched and Mk. 3 fixed-wing-launched versions. It is being carried here by a RNorAF F-16A. (NFT)

► Following manufacturer's trials in the United States in October 1990, BAeD released this shot of an Alarm passing close to a target on the US Naval Weapons Center range at China Lake. The missile was equipped with a telemetry head for the trial, but had a warhead been in place the target would have been destroyed. (BAeD)

booster rockets and auxiliary fins of the coastal or ship-launched version but is otherwise similar. Trials have begun on a AJ.37 Viggen and it will, eventually, arm the JAS.39 Gripen.

This chapter has highlighted the variety of air armament available today, together with glimpses into the future. Although it does not claim to be totally comprehensive in its coverage, it does show the way. For the distant future, we may consider the use of directed laser-energy weapons and even sonic systems, but guns, rockets, bombs and missiles, including a decreasing but more capable nuclear element, will be with us for many years to come. To summarize, one can say that modern aircraft armament covers a broad spectrum but that it also needs more than the element that 'goes bang'. It must be designed with the specific type of target and weapons platform in mind and that integration of weapon and aircraft system must begin as early as possible, before metal is cut or composite formed. Proven, as much as new, technology must play a part. For the next century, Captain Strange's dictum could be re-written as 'Every man who goes into the air in a fighting machine is a weapons-aimer – first and last!'.

The ultimate test for any combat aircraft – and this broad description includes the vast spectrum of aircraft involved in support roles mentioned in the early chapters – is war. Most recently, this has been the United Nations coalition war against Iraq, early in 1991. It has been referred to throughout this book in specific instances, to illustrate various points.

It is often said that combat equipment, be it guns, tanks, warships or aircraft, is always designed to fight the last war, whatever and wherever that was. The result is that many systems and items of equipment have to fight in a war role for which they were never actually designed, and in a region where it was never planned that they should be deployed. The truth of the first statement has been gradually diluted during the 1980s, while the truth of the second was confirmed by the Gulf War.

It is still too early to master all the implications of the Gulf War: virtually none of the air arms involved has itself completed a detailed review. The full circumstances of every mission are not, and may never be, made public. The so-called 'blue-on-blue' incident, where a USAF A-10 destroyed two British Warrior infantry fighting vehicles, is but one unfortunate (and emotional) example. However hard it may seem on the friends and relatives of the deceased in this case, it must be acknowledged that this was war. All soldiers, sailors and airmen are human, and mistakes *do* happen. This incident was a tragic mistake but, had the overall casualties in the war been higher, it is doubtful that the incident would have attracted the media attention it received.

It is, however, possible to draw some initial conclusions based on clear-cut, well-reported facts. If any of the following appear as a blinding glimpse of the obvious, I would apologize to the reader, while reminding him or her that many lessons of previous wars and conflicts have invariably to be re-learnt on the field of battle. The 'corporate memory' of the general public and, in many instances, of the politicians responsible for initiating a military action, is notoriously short. So, to be positive, what lessons did the Gulf War offer us, and how may they affect the way ahead?

One concept that the USAF has already initiated as a result of the Gulf experience has been that of 'mixed Wings'. It has been noted that in order to get one formation of strike aircraft over the target, it took a whole mixture of varying support types – reconnaissance aircraft, escort EW jammers, defence-suppression aircraft (Wild Weasels), aerial tankers and fighter escorts, plus helicopters and back-up combat types to attempt the rescue of any air crew who may have abandoned damaged or destroyed aircraft. Taking it one stage beyond, there is the pyramid of air transport forces used to assist the deployment of the aircraft and their support into the region before, during and after the war.

The success of the EW employed in the Gulf War was unparalleled and, as a result, one suspects that this element is receiving much attention to improve its effectiveness. By way of example, the author has been told by industry sources in the UK that over 25 per cent of the expenditure of Operation 'Granby', the UK element of Operations 'Desert Shield/Storm' and 'Desert Sabre', was devoted to improving the EW capability of RAF aircraft deployed in the theatre of operations. However, this is one of the more sensitive issues in combat aviation, and much remains secret. The US Navy is considering re-opening the EA-6B Prowler production line, while the USAF's F-4G Wild Weasels are to be retained in service (with appropriate extension of life, where necessary) until a dedicated replacement solution to the requirement can be fielded.

Much to the amazement of the public (and, one suspects, of the politicians) was the way in which the so-called 'smart' weapons launched against varying types of targets worked 'as advertised'. When the laser-guided bomb went down the air vent of a specified target in Baghdad, how many television viewers were put in mind of the attack sequence in the film *Star Wars*? Science fiction became science fact that day – and forget about 'using the Force, Luke'! The reality is that, especially in the United States, such weapons have to be tested and evaluated at so many stages in their development and entry into service that, of course, they will work – most of the time. By the same token, identified military targets can be destroyed without the vast collateral damage associated with, say, 1,000 bombers over Germany in the Second World War. Again, it must be said that mistakes can happen: witness the attack on the Baghdad air-raid shelter that may or may not at one time have been a command post of some description. At the end of the war, one of the points made by the BBC's reporter John Simpson was that there were no massive areas of civilian damage in the city.

It is also true to say that there is nothing like a war to enable the services to cut through the bureaucratic red tape of procurement procedure to get what they want.

THE WAY AHEAD

In Britain we saw it work miraculously during the Falklands conflict, and so it was, again, during the Gulf War. The classic example was probably the development of the airborne early warning version of the Sea King helicopter. With the advent of the generation of aircraft carriers (at one stage in their development known as 'through-deck cruisers', for political purposes) which carried only Sea Harrier STOVL combat aircraft, the Royal Navy acknowledged it had no replacement for the Gannet AEW.3. Thorn EMI and Westland had developed a concept of what became the Sea King AEW.2A three years before the Falklands campaign. When the conflict erupted these plans were 'rediscovered' and dusted down and, within ten weeks, the first two modified Sea Kings sailed with HMS *Illustrious* to the South Atlantic.

Similarly, it took the Falklands War to hammer home the need for individual comprehensive EW systems on aircraft and the fitting of decoy dispensers to offer a last-ditch defence against incoming SAMs of whatever description. At least this lesson was not lost on the RAF. When, in 1988, the author flew in an operational Tornado F.3 fighter, he made the observation in an initial draft of his article (which had to be cleared by the MoD as a condition of the flight being sanctioned) that the Tornado F.3 did not have any chaff/flare dispensers. This direct criticism, which could have been made by anyone looking at an F.3 at a public air show, was 'red-pencilled' by a nameless person within the MoD. On challenge, a form of words which made the point, but less directly, was agreed and published. One of the first modifications made to the Tornado F.3s deployed to the Gulf in 1990 was the addition of a chaff/flare dispenser. Depending on one's viewpoint, one could say that the Treasury's budget limitations did not permit the earlier installation of such equipment or that the RAF did not place sufficient priority on such measures. The truth lies somewhere between the two extremes, and it is now known that installation was planned as part of a mid-life update for the aircraft. The list of such examples is, if not endless, certainly very long. The reality of defence procurement, despite the 'blip' of the Gulf War, is that budgets are reducing as the public clamours for the so-called 'peace dividend'. When specifying a new aircraft or weapon, someone has to draw the line between the 'must have' and the 'nice to have' capabilities. It is no easy task but, if one believes the politicians, parallel with force reductions will be equipment improvements.

The results of a recent study into the European Fighter Aircraft's effectiveness against an improved Soviet Sukhoi Su-27 (sometimes referred to as 'Son of Flanker' – its NATO codename) show an 82 per cent chance of success in a one-on-one BVR engagement. To achieve that result a sum of money is being expended. The YF-22 plotted into the same scenario shows a 91 per cent chance of success – but at a cost at least three or four times greater than that of EFA. Any air force will want to get the best equipment it can afford, but it must also balance its books and, therefore, declare priorities. 'Smaller but better' may be the ideal but, if followed to its logical conclusion, it must be accepted that the 'peace dividend' is not going to materialize in the short term.

So, if nothing else, one trend has emerged. When a combat aircraft for tomorrow is being designed, one can no longer make a sketch on the back of the proverbial envelope and translate that on to the drawing board, taking the necessary equipment and powerplant 'off the shelf'. The ultimate role of the combat aircraft must be subordinate to the weapon which it needs to accomplish that role. At long last, some common sense is beginning to prevail – yet it has not gone as far as some individual air staff officers, obliged to think ten or more years ahead, would like.

The US forces have an established procedure which is now a vital hurdle in the development of any weapons system – the Mission Elements Need Statement or MENS. In simple terms, this outlines the task that the end-product, be it gun, tank, warship or aircraft, is required to perform. How this is achieved is down to the contractor in liaison with the customer. The UK has its Cardinal Points System, but this is as much directed towards competitive tendering (getting value for money) as ensuring that the services get exactly what they need.

The element which has not yet been touched upon, of course, is that of political influence. It took the RAF from 1977 to 1986 and £930 million wasted on Nimrod AEW.3 to get approval for the aircraft it knew it wanted for its airborne early warning task – the E-3 Sentry AWACS. Now, as the first RAF Sentries enter service, replacing 'interim' Shackleton AEW.2 aircraft, it should be noted that the scandal of the Nimrod AEW.3 was not so much the inability of the radar contractor to deliver a system that performed as required but rather the poor standard of project management at MoD level combined with the bureaucracy of the Civil Service.

International politics can also bring its problems. The rising costs of combat aircraft have dictated collaborative ventures. Partners have to be found, and their air staffs must then agree what must, perforce, be a compromise air staff target and refine it. Invariably, the result will have to be all things to all air forces. This requirement must then be put out to tender within the industries of the countries, whether they be formed as consortia or not, and contracts must be awarded so that each country's overall share of the project is maintained.

What effect will this have on the aircraft itself? Simply that all eventualities will be investigated, evaluated and covered. Even acknowledging the advances of technology, with one or two exceptions the combat aircraft and helicopters of the twenty-first century will not look very dissimilar from those in service today. The conservatism of many air forces will ensure that this is so. The author's 'gut reaction' that the YF-22 would be the type selected by the USAF for its ATF requirement was based as much on the fact that it looked more like the F-15 it will replace than did the YF-23 as on the technical advances made by the manufacturers. Evolution in shape will happen but at nowhere like the rate illustrators of future projects (or science fiction comics) would have us believe.

This is not to discount the technical advances that have been made and, indeed, are being made as these words are read. For example, if all the signs are interpreted correctly, the AX replacement for the US Navy's cancelled A-12 will be less evolutionary in looks. The fact is that radar stealth is not the only function within the overall picture. Electro-optical systems (specifically IRST) are fast becoming more sensitive and are achieving, therefore, detections equal to those by radar but on differing parameters. The author has been told that one system exists which is quite capable of picking out the F-117 simply on the basis of the contrast between the temperature of the aircraft and that of the surrounding air, despite its low radar cross-section.

These very advances can take an old aircraft and give it a new lease of life beyond the wildest dreams of the designer. The McDonnell Douglas A-4 Skyhawk first flew in 1954. Today, Singapore is re-engining its A-4s and giving them a new suite of avionics which will see an effective life of 50 years for the Skyhawk design. This process of system modernization, mid-life update or service life extension – whichever of the appropriate 'buzz phrases' are in vogue – has become a fact of life. Such a process can not only improve the effectiveness of the aircraft's operation and ease the maintenance involved, it can also reduce its life-cycle costs, to say nothing of the costs involved in procuring replacements.

Technology has also seen some ideas and concepts which were ahead of their time begin to become feasible – in terms of cost and effectiveness. The remotely piloted aircraft, drone or (the latest expression) unmanned air vehicle has proved of immense value in reconnaissance and surveillance for all three arms of the services, but only because the systems have been refined as a result of the key technologies covered in an earlier chapter. Likewise, the airship is beginning a renaissance. In the companion volume to this, *Sea Power 2000*, Bernard Ireland talks about the US Navy's YEZ-2 Sentinel 5000 airship being developed by Westinghouse of the US and Airship Industries in the UK. With the demise of the British company, Westinghouse has taken over the project entirely and, although the US Navy still has overall management, the driving force has become the American Air Defense Initiative. A radar with a large aperture can be housed inside the envelope of the airship, making it possible to detect targets which more conventional AEW aircraft just cannot pick up. While the potential for ASW remains, the surveillance role is taking over in priority.

So, if aircraft are getting cleverer and can be, within specific categories, truly multi-role, what benefits can accrue to air forces? Foremost is the reduction in the number of different types of aircraft needed to conduct the air force's designated roles. For the RAF, the Tornado GR.1 has replaced the Vulcan bomber, many Buccaneer strike aircraft and some Jaguar strike and reconnaissance aircraft. The Buccaneers will have finally gone by 1994. The Tornado F.3 has taken over from the venerable Lightning and many of the Phantoms in the air defence role. The last Phantoms will go by the end of 1992. The Harriers have been replaced by the second-generation Harrier II and, from the late 1990s, EFA will replace the remaining Jaguars and complement (if not totally replace) the Tornado F.3. The savings in maintenance costs and logistics support can be tremendous. Operationally, the ability to swing from one role to another in a relatively short time offers great flexibility when, in the past, another aircraft type would have had to be deployed to cover an emerging requirement. The trap which such advantages can lead an air force to fall into is the one of fleet size versus mission demands. Even with a smaller, multi-role combat fleet, there must be sufficient numbers of these aircraft to allow the tasks allocated to the military by the politicians to be adequately covered.

This prompts the question 'What is the threat?'. For more than forty years, the cornerstone of Western defence philosophy has been the potential of the Soviet Union and her Warsaw Pact allies to launch an attack in Central Europe from, virtually, a standing start. This premise is now dead: the Warsaw Pact is dissolved, and newly independent European states have emerged as effective 'buffers'. Yet what we knew as the Soviet Union still retains a vast arsenal and, despite the reductions imposed by the Conventional Forces in Europe treaty, a Soviet threat has not entirely disappeared, especially on the northern and southern flanks of NATO.

To gaze into the proverbial crystal ball, it would appear that the major threat to world peace, as perceived in the early years after the dissolution of the Warsaw Pact, is of out-of-area (to NATO) conflicts from totally unexpected sources. We return to the Gulf War as a prime example, although the Falklands War or the French operations in Chad would be equally applicable. Religious or racial divisions may well fuel such conflicts. To this end, NATO is to reorganize itself to create a Rapid Reaction Corps to respond to such eventualities. Although it did not happen in the Gulf, it is not beyond the bounds of possibility to foresee the former protagonists of East and West join forces, literally, against a common, as yet unknown enemy.

The closer ties within Europe are also beginning to see a new power base. The way in which EC nations have strived to resolve the racial conflict within Yugoslavia (yet to be settled at the time of writing) is indicative of both the problems and the benefits of such closeness. That said, we are still many years away from a European Defence Force – despite the Franco-German proposals.

At present, it seems as if every major defence and aerospace company is searching for joint ventures or collaboration, either against specific national or international requirements or purely in an effort to pool resources and reduce costs. There is now no doubt that international (specifically European) collaboration can work (witness Jaguar, Tornado and now EFA); while within the United States, the number of new projects has necessitated 'teaming'. The sophistication of new military aerospace projects means that both development and production costs are rising, and collaboration splits the overall R&D costs down into company- or country-manageable packets. Production costs can be a different matter.

When EFA was initiated, a production run of almost 800 aircraft was required. This could now drop to as few as 400 (not counting exports beyond the four participating countries). This commercially horrifying reality must have corporate accountants working overtime on their calculators. However, in the case of EFA, a representative of one partner company was quite categoric in his assertion that the target of an average price for EFA (of £21 million, in 1991 pounds) could be achieved at this lower figure of 400 aircraft. This, he maintained, was the result of firm, fixed-price contracting on the project. While the author has no access to figures which would confirm or disprove the statement, it must be admitted that, while hoping it to be true, he remains sceptical.

However, it would be fair to state that, on the whole, while collaboration can bring reduced R&D costs to individual companies or countries, there is a limit to the reduction in production costs. What matters is that they remain acceptable to, and affordable by, the customer – leaving exports (fast becoming a political 'hot potato' in some countries) to provide the 'icing on the cake'.

Air power is changing. In some areas it is changing very rapidly, in others more slowly. It is a function of the perennial conflict between conservatism and innovation. Right now, we are seeing the effects of a modern air war impacting on long-held and, sometimes, inertia-bound thinking. There is no doubt that benefits will accrue from the experience. However, it will remain a 'blip' in the graph. The truth that 'to jaw-jaw is better than war-war' has never been more important. Perhaps we are approaching, or have even turned, the corner where man's baser instincts cause him to resort to violence. The choice of where and when to fight a war is rarely in the hands of the military. They must fight today's, and tomorrow's, war with what they have at the present, not what is due in service in three years' time. As we move towards the twenty-first century, air power maintains its vital part in warfare. Churchill also once said that 'It is practically impossible to win an argument with someone who is unencumbered by knowledge of the facts'. This book has endeavoured to explain some of those basic facts as they relate to Air Power in the year 2000.

Analog(ue) A physical object or quantity, such as a pointer (indicator arm) on a dial instrument, used to measure or represent another quantity.

Analog(ue) computer Electronic computer in which input data are continuous varying values operated upon as corresponding electrical voltages.

AOA Angle of attack (sometimes referred to as 'alpha' or 'angle of incidence'). The angle between the wing chord line (from the leading to trailing edge of the wing) and the local undisturbed airflow direction.

BAI Battlefield Air Interdiction. Air-launched strikes to the rear of the battlefield, concentrating on immediate reinforcements for the land battle.

Boresight To align a gun or other device by means of optical sighting on a target.

BVR Beyond Visual Range.

Canard A tail-first aircraft, usually with auxiliary horizontal control surfaces at the front (foreplanes) but a vertical surface (fin and rudder) at rear. Sometimes the foreplane is referred to as the canard.

CAP Combat Air Patrol.

CAS Close Air Support. The modern expression for ground attack against enemy forces engaging own troops.

Casevac Casualty Evacuation.

CATH Common Anti-Tank Helicopter. A programme name for two of the three variants of what is now the Eurocopter Tiger programme being developed jointly by France and Germany.

Clutter Unwanted returns on a display, usually radar, caused by atmospheric interference, lightning, natural static, hostile ECM or ground or sea returns.

CFC Carbon Fibre Composite.

Composite (material) Structural material made up of two or more contrasting components, normally fine fibres in a bonding matrix. Unlike an alloy, usually of a fibreglass form.

DFCS Digital Flight Control System, whereby pilot control input is converted into electronic signals and transmitted by wire to the control surface, where it is translated back into a physical movement of the control surface.

Digital Operating on discrete numbers, bits or other individual packets of information.

Dunk To lower into the water on a tether or cable.

Dunking sonar A sonar system where the antenna is lowered into the water from a helicopter in order to detect submarines.

ECCM Electronic counter-countermeasures.

ECM Electronic countermeasures.

Elint Electronic intelligence. Any form of intelligence (knowledge) gained by electronic means.

EMP Electro-Magnetic Pulse. Caused by the detonation of a nuclear device which can interfere with or black out electronic signals of all types within a defined area.

ESM Electronic support measures. A non-active (i.e. passive) means of detecting hostile electronic surveillance.

FBW Fly-by-wire. The common term for digital flying controls.

Fenestron The tail-rotor system of a helicopter 'buried' within the tail structure. Coined by the French manufacturer Aérospatiale. The US equivalent on the RAH-66A Comanche is known as 'fan-in-fin'.

FLIR Forward-looking infra red (system).

FOL Forward Operating Location. An austere base where combat aircraft can refuel and re-arm during a battle.

FGA Fighter, Ground Attack.

GPS Global Positioning System, which uses US-launched satellites to give exact navigation fixes to aircraft, helicopters, ships or the land vehicles of troops.

HOTAS Hands On Throttle And Stick. The basic controls a pilot needs to fly and fight his aircraft may all be concentrated on the throttle and control column (stick) and thus do not require him to move his hands from these two vital controls during air combat.

Interceptor A fighter aircraft designed to intercept and if necessary destroy other aircraft.

Interdictor A strike or bomber aircraft which attacks tactical targets deep in hostile territory, well beyond a battle area or front line.

IRST Infra-Red Search and Track. A passive device using an infra-red seeker to locate targets without transmitting energy.

Jet tab A small power-operated flap, spoiler or ring on the skirt or nozzle of a rocket or engine exhaust used for thrust-vectoring control.

LERX Leading-edge root extension. Used to improve the aerodynamic control of an aircraft at high angles of attack.

MAD Magnetic Anomaly Detector. A device which detects disturbances in the Earth's natural magnetic field. Used for detecting submarines.

MANPADS Man-Portable Air Defence System. A one-man, shoulder-launched or two-man, portable surface-to-air missile, without radar surveillance and tracking.

Medevac Medical Evacuation. US equivalent of Casevac.

MEP Mission Equipment Package. Usually refers to sensor-/processor and display equipment designed for a specific role.

Monopulse Radar technique using overlapping pencil-beams, two for azimuth, two for elevation, with circuitry arranged so that, when the target is centralized with the beams, the output voltage vanishes.

NOTAR No tail rotor. The proprietary name for a helicopter anti-torque tail control system, developed by the McDonnell Douglas Helicopter Company in the US, which uses deflected engine exhaust ducted to the rear of the tail structure.

Paddle blades (rotor) 1. The enlarged tips of helicopter main rotor blades, developed as part of the British Rotorcraft Experimental Programme (BERP) and sometimes known as BERP-tips. 2. External 'rudders' mounted outside the main engine exhaust and used as thrust deflectors as on the X-31 EFM demonstrator aircraft.

PCB Plenum Chamber Burning. A form of afterburning used to increase thrust on vectored-thrust engines.

Pintle mount A cantilever type of pivot-pin gun mounting, used mainly on helicopters and light aircraft.

Pre-preg Composite fibres or fibre matting pre-impregnated with resin which, when heat-treated in an autoclave oven, produces a solid composite structure.

QRA Quick Reaction Alert. An RAF/NATO term referring to (usually) a pair of interceptor fighters kept at a high state of readiness, close to the main runway so that they can be launched against an incoming, potentially hostile target in the minimum time.

RAM Radar Absorbent Material.

RAS 1. Radar Absorbent Structure. 2. Replenishment At Sea. A technique for passing non-liquid stores, usually from a supply vessel to a warship, at sea while both vessels are under way (cf. Vertrep).

Rudderatrons A US expression for the control surface on flying-wing aircraft – which would, on a conventional tailed aircraft, be the ailerons – providing control in the rolling plane, but on a flying wing are being used also to control the aircraft in the yawing plane.

Ruddervator A term to describe the control surfaces used in place of the rudders on the fin and elevators on the tail-plane when both control surfaces are merged into a 'butterfly tail' configuration.

Sidelobe A lobe of aerial radiation (usually radar) propagated at an angle to the main lobe, usually unwanted and often the cause of clutter or false returns.

Sigint Signals intelligence. Specific information gained from the interception of radio and data communications.

SLAR Sideways-looking airborne radar. Used for surveillance, the antenna is located down the aircraft centreline, radiating at 90 degrees to the track on one side or both sides (depending on aerial configuration).

STOVL Short Take-Off, Vertical Landing. A practical and more accurate representation of the operational use of Harrier-type aircraft than the initial V/STOL (Vertical or Short Take-Off and Landing). Using a short take-off, more payload can be carried, while at the end of a mission, with weapons and most of the fuel expended, the aircraft is light enough to land vertically.

TARPS Tactical Air Reconnaissance Pod System.

Thrust-vectoring Rotating of the thrust line in order to move an aircraft's or missile's trajectory.

Transient 1. Temporary surge in a variable, such as the initial swtiching on of equipment. 2. Electrical impulse of short duration repeated irregularly.

Turbojet The simplest form of gas turbine, comprising a compressor, combustion chamber and turbine (extracting sufficient energy to drive the compressor). Most of the energy remains as gas, exhausted through a propelling nozzle, where afterburning can be installed.

Turbofan A more efficient propulsion system than a turbojet, consisting of a gas turbine core engine with extra turbine stages (usually on a low-pressure shaft) driving a large-diameter fan, which ducts a large propulsive airflow around the core engine and generates most of the thrust. For a given fuel consumption, the turbofan generates more take-off thrust than a turbojet and much less noise.

Turboprop Similar to a turbofan but with extra turbine power, geared down, to drive a propeller.

Turboshaft Essentially a turbofan or turboprop (with fan or propeller removed, as appropriate) geared to deliver shaft power to helicopters or air cushion vehicles. Can often deliver power from both ends and usually has a speed-reducing gearbox.

Vertrep A specific form of replenishment at sea (see RAS) using helicopters to transfer cargo from one vessel to another.

INDEX